WORD 2000

in easy steps

SCOTT BASHAM

COMPUTER STEP

In easy steps is an imprint of Computer Step
Southfield Road . Southam
Warwickshire CV47 OFB . England

http://www.ineasysteps.com

Notice of Liability

Every effort has been made to ensure that this book contains accurate
and current information. However, Computer Step and the author shall
not be liable for any loss or damage suffered by readers as a result of
any information contained herein.

Trademarks

Microsoft® and Windows® are registered trademarks of Microsoft
Corporation. All other trademarks are acknowledged as belonging to
their respective companies.

Printed and bound in the United Kingdom

ISBN 1-84078-037-1

Table Of Contents

5 Styles and Themes — 63

6 Tabulation — 77

7 Automatic Features — 83

Getting to Know Word

This chapter gets you started with Word 2000 quickly. It explains the screen layout, and introduces the various viewing modes that you can use to display your documents. It looks at new Word 2000 features, such as its personalised menus and docking toolbars, and the extensive Help facilities.

Covers

Chapter One

Introduction

Word-processing was one of the first popular applications for the modern personal computer. In the early days it provided little more than the ability to enter and change text on a computer monitor. As time went on software and hardware improved, and features such as spell-checking and various type effects were added. The number of users increased.

Microsoft Word 2000 for Windows is widely acknowledged as a leader in its field, and is one of the best selling packages in any software category.

Let's face it, with Word 2000 we're talking about a *big* package. It has retained the position as market leader by stuffing itself full of useful features, taking it from word-processing into the realms of graphical and data-oriented documents, and adding the capacity for Internet communications. At first it may seem to contain a bewildering array of options and controls, but many are there to make life easier – providing quick access to the most commonly used features.

A big package sometimes comes with a depressingly big reference manual, which will describe each and every function in minute detail. This book is not intended to replace the manual; instead you should view it as a more graphical teaching guide. Wherever possible, pictures and examples are used rather than pages of text to explain and demonstrate the concepts covered.

To gain maximum benefit from this book:

- Make sure that you are first familiar with the Windows operating environment (i.e. using a Mouse, icons, menus, dialog boxes etc.).

- It is important to experiment using your own examples; like many things you will find that practice is the key to competence.

The Word 2000 Screen

Start Word by selecting Programs>Microsoft Word from the Start menu. You should see the following screen:

Title and Document bar   Menus   Ruler

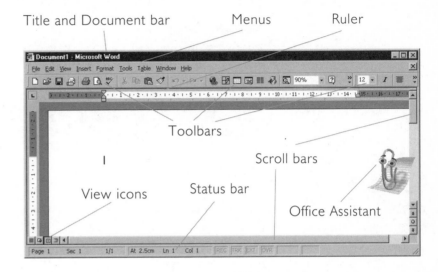

Toolbars

Scroll bars

View icons   Status bar

Office Assistant

Don't worry if the screen you see has extra items or things missing; you'll see in a moment that it's possible to configure the Word 2000 screen in different ways.

Toolbars

Toolbars can appear at the top of the screen, at the bottom, or as floating palettes. They give you instant access to features without the need to search through menus and dialog boxes. There are sixteen toolbars in total, but we usually only require several at any time.

Activating/Deactivating Toolbars

To quickly activate a toolbar, right-click the Mouse on any currently visible toolbar to display a shortcut menu (see opposite). Check the toolbar of your choice.

To deactivate a toolbar, follow the same procedure, but instead uncheck the toolbar in the pop-up menu.

1   Go to the View menu and choose "Toolbars".

2   In this example we've switched off all except for "Standard" and "Formatting".

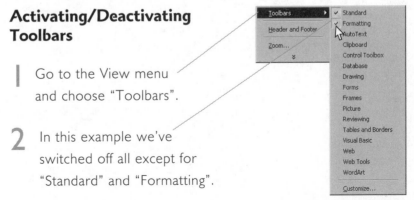

Page Views

There are four different ways of viewing the page, which you can select from the top section of the View menu: *Normal, Web Layout, Print Layout, and Outline.*

Normal View

This view allows fast editing, previewing most text effects, but does not display images and other objects.

The quickest way to switch views is to use the icons in the bottom left corner of the screen.

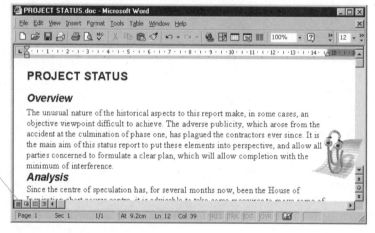

Web Layout View

This makes online reading easier by displaying text larger than it would print, and by displaying the Document Map, a tool you can use to move easily through your document.

In any of these views, paragraph symbols (markers denoting carriage returns, spaces, etc.) are by default not visible. To display them, click on the Paragraph Symbols icon normally displayed in the Standard toolbar:

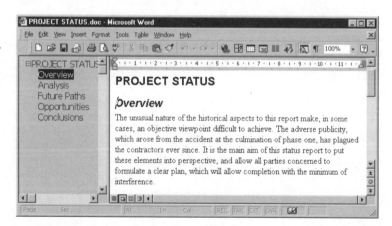

...cont'd

Print Layout View

This view displays your document as actual pages, previewing text and graphics effects.

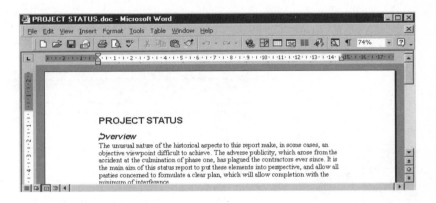

Outline View

This allows you to view your text as a structured outline. Each major heading is marked with a plus-sign; subordinate headings are marked with a minus sign. To collapse a heading so that subordinate headings are not displayed, double-click on the plus-sign.

The structure of a document can be rearranged from Outline view by dragging the plus- and minus-signs to another part of the document.

In previous versions of Word, there was an additional Master Document View. In Word 2000 this has been merged with Outline View.

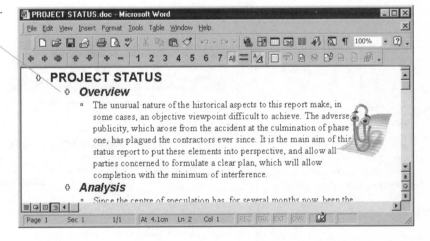

Customising the Toolbars

You can configure Word's Toolbars in a wide variety of ways.

Moving Toolbars

Move to the left edge of a toolbar. Your pointer should turn into a double arrow as shown below.

Start dragging here

If you drag a floating toolbar back to the top of the screen, it will reattach itself to the toolbar area.

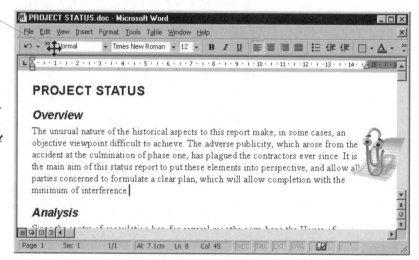

If you drag onto the main page area, the toolbar will become "free and floating".

You close down a floating toolbar by clicking on the cross in its top right corner. You can later reactivate it from the View menu or by right-clicking on any other toolbar.

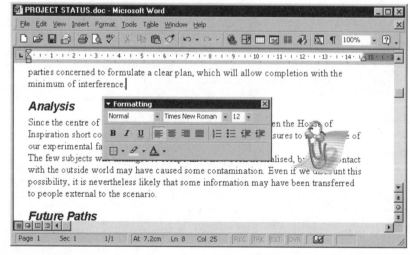

Accessing extra Toolbar buttons

If a toolbar is too small to display all its icons, then you can still access them by clicking on the ⇒ icon.

Click here

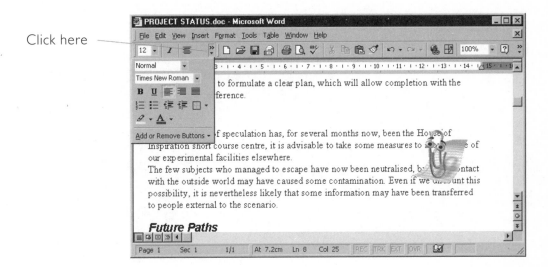

Resizing Toolbars

You can resize a toolbar by dragging on its right hand edge. Your pointer will turn into a double arrow when you are in the right place to begin dragging.

Drag from here

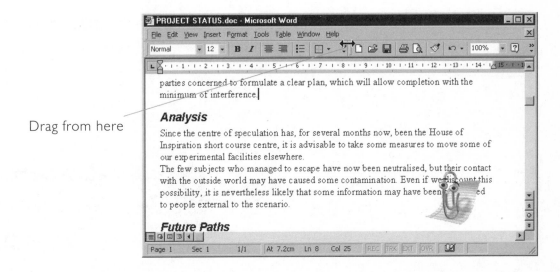

Adding or Removing Buttons

Each toolbar has a control marked "Add or Remove Buttons". If you can't see this, then click on the ⋙ symbol in the toolbar.

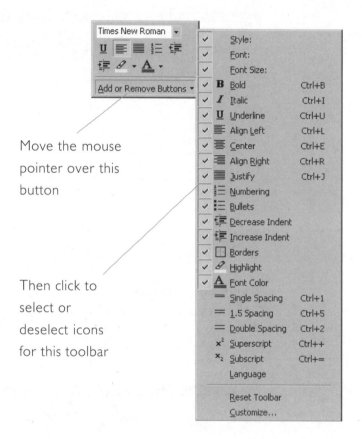

Move the mouse pointer over this button

Then click to select or deselect icons for this toolbar

You can also add and remove buttons from a floating toolbar.

Click here to access the pop-up menu

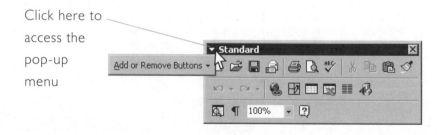

Adjusting the Page Setup

Go to the File menu and choose "Page Setup". The Page Setup dialog box appears. Like many of Word's dialog boxes, it is *tabbed*, i.e. subdivided into sections. You can select your required section by clicking on the appropriate tab at the top of the box.

1 Make sure the Margins tab is selected.

2 Type in any required changes to the margin or header/footer dimensions.

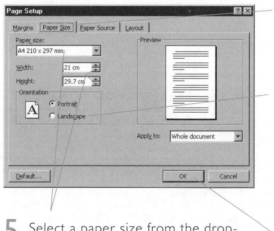

3 Click on the Paper Size tab.

4 Select a page orientation: Portrait (tall) or Landscape (wide).

You can also select tabs by pressing the Alt key together with the underlined letter in the tab name.

Alternatively, pressing Control together with the Tab key itself will cycle through each tab in turn.

5 Select a paper size from the drop-down list, or enter custom values in the Width and Height boxes.

6 Make any necessary changes in the Paper Source and Layout tabs.

7 Click "OK" to apply your changes.

Help

Word 2000 features several basic ways of offering you help. In increasing order of sophistication, these are Help boxes, context sensitive help, and (for users of Microsoft Office 2000) the Office Assistant.

Help Boxes

If you allow your Mouse pointer to rest over an icon for a moment, a Help box will appear. This gives you a brief explanation of the icon's function.

Help box ——

Context Sensitive Help

1 Go to the Help menu and choose "What's This?".

The pointer turns into an arrow with a question mark attached until the next time you click.

2 Move your pointer to the element in which you're interested, then click. You can also open a menu to see help describing a particular option.

The keyboard shortcut for context sensitive help is Shift + F1.

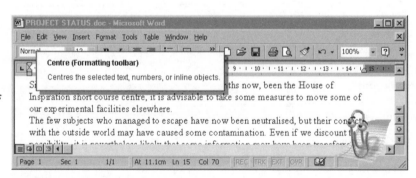

A pop-up box will appear, with a description of the item or menu option.

The Assistant

The Assistant is a "delightful" animated character who is always eager to provide you with help.

If the Assistant isn't already displayed, select Show the Office Assistant from the Help menu. When the Assistant is active, this menu option becomes Hide the Office Assistant.

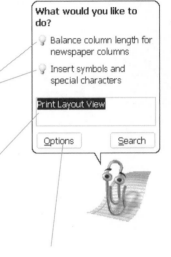

1 To get help, click on the Assistant. A window appears.

2 Click one of the lightbulb icons to see suggested help information. The Assistant bases this on what you're currently doing.

3 Alternatively, enter some text relating to the information you want, then click "Search".

4 Click "Options" to set preferences for the Assistant.

If you click on the Assistant with your right Mouse button, then a pop-up Menu appears.

Changing the Assistant

One day far into the future you may tire of your Office Assistant. Here's how to sack him/her and select another.

> Right click on the Assistant and select "Choose Assistant" from the pop-up menu.

To change the Assistant, you will probably be asked to insert your Office CD.

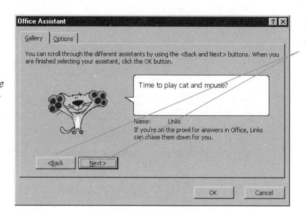

2 Click on these buttons to cycle through the different Assistants, then click "OK".

Smart Menus

When you initially open a menu, Word will show you an abbreviated list of options containing only those which are frequently used.

Any options you have used recently will automatically be added to the short menu. This way Word adapts to your working methods, so that commands you need are always within easy reach.

If you keep it open for a few moments, or click on the ⊻ option at the bottom of the abbreviated menu, then you'll see the full menu. (Notice that the lesser-used features are shown in a paler grey.)

Basic Text Manipulation

This chapter helps you start entering and manipulating text on the screen. It looks at different ways of editing and formatting type, as well as saving and printing your work.

Covers

Chapter Two

The Document Window

The New
Document icon

| If there is no Document window, then create a new one by clicking on the "New" icon in the top left of the standard toolbar.

2 Enter a sentence of example text.

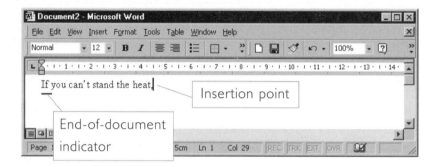

The vertical line is your *insertion point*, indicating where new text will appear. You can move the insertion point by:

- Using the cursor (arrow) keys.

- Clicking a new position with the Mouse.

Word automatically works out when to take a new line without breaking words. If you want to start a new paragraph, press the Return or Enter key.

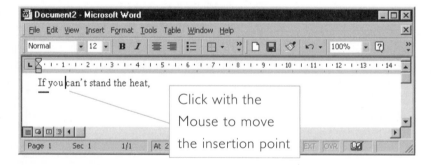

Inserting Text

| Move the insertion point to a point where you would like to add more text.

2 Type the text. It will appear at the insertion point.

Note that the words to the right of the insertion point move along to accommodate the new text:

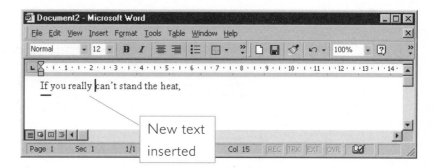

Deleting Text Using Backspace

Move the insertion point so that it is directly after the text you want to delete.

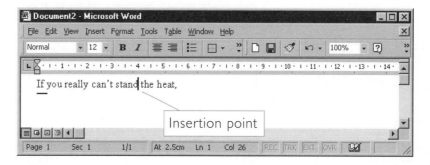

2 Press the Backspace key once to erase each character to the *left* of the insertion point.

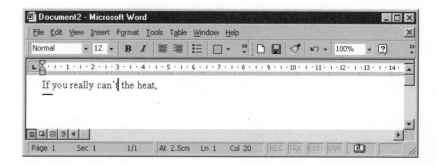

Deleting Text with the Delete Key

This time move the insertion point before the text to be deleted.

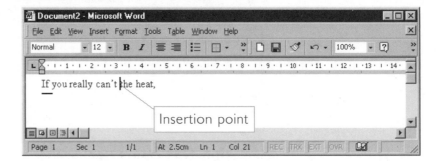

Insertion point

Press the Delete key once to erase each character to the *right* of the insertion point.

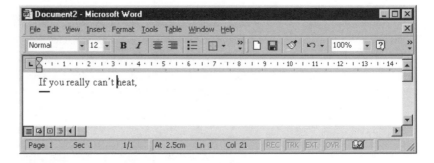

Selecting Text

You can select text by using the Mouse to drag horizontally across it, while holding down the left button:

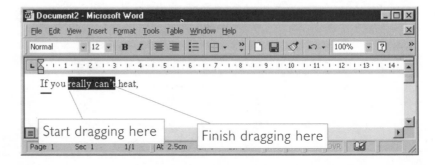

Start dragging here   Finish dragging here

Replacing Selected Text

Anything you type will automatically replace any text which is currently selected:

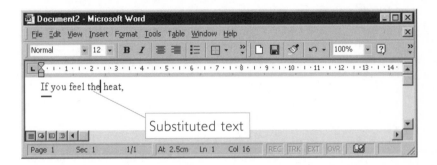

Adding More Text to the End of the Document

1 Remember that before adding more text to the end of your document you must first reposition the insertion point:

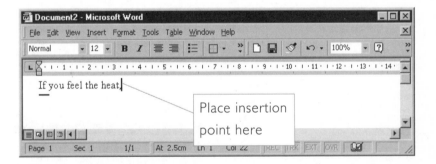

2 Add the text:

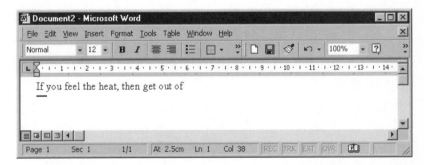

Insert versus Overtype

At the bottom of the screen, in the Status bar, the letters "OVR" should be greyed out. This indicates that you are in Insert, rather than Overtype mode.

1 Double-click the "OVR" indicator.

The text in the "OVR" indicator will turn black, showing that Overtype mode is selected. In Overtype mode, new text overtypes (replaces) any text to the right of the insertion point, instead of shifting the old text to the right.

2 Position the insertion point somewhere within your text:

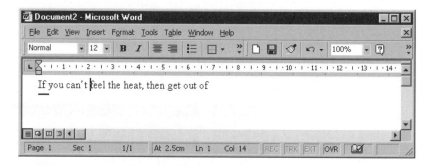

3 Type some new text.

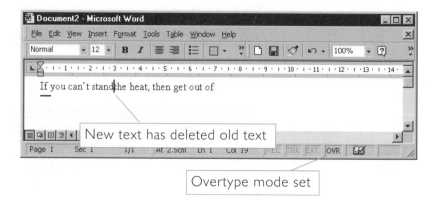

New text has deleted old text

Overtype mode set

4 Double-click once more on the "OVR" indicator to switch back to Insert mode.

Selecting All the Text in a Document

Choose the "Select All" option from the Edit Menu (or press Ctrl+A).

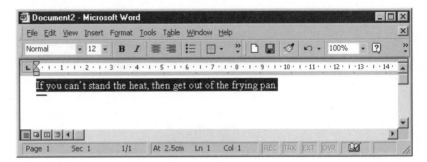

Changing the Appearance of Text

With all the text selected, open the "Size" pop-up menu from the toolbar, and increase the point size of the text to around twice the previous value.

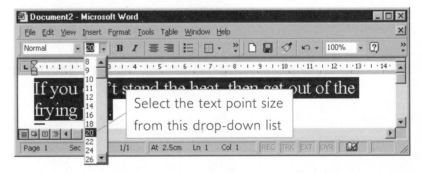

Select the text point size from this drop-down list

2 Select a single word. Use the toolbar to switch on the Bold effect.

The keyboard shortcut for Bold is Control+Shift+B.

Click here to switch Bold on and off

3 If you want to select text over more than one line, either drag over the area required or click at one end of the selection, then hold down Shift and click at the other end:

4 You can also select whole lines of text by dragging vertically over the area within the left margin.

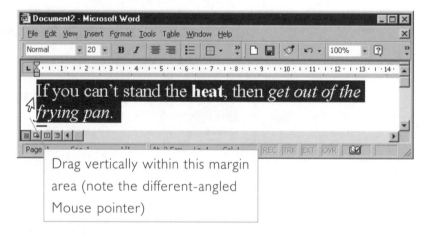

5 Alternatively, you can double-click to select a single word, or triple-click to select an entire paragraph.

6 Note that if you click an insertion point and then type more text, the new text takes its attributes (appearance) from the previous character:

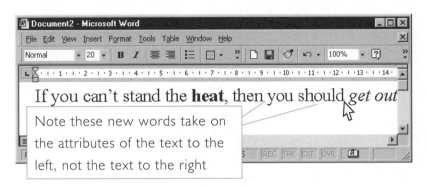

> Note these new words take on the attributes of the text to the left, not the text to the right

Click and Type

This is a time saving feature, new to Word 2000. If you are in Print Layout or Web Layout view you can add text virtually anywhere on the page. Simply double-click to establish an insertion point.

If Click and Type doesn't appear to work, then first make sure that you're in Print Layout or Web Layout view. Then open the Tools menu and choose Options. Select the Edit tab and make sure that Click and Type is activated.

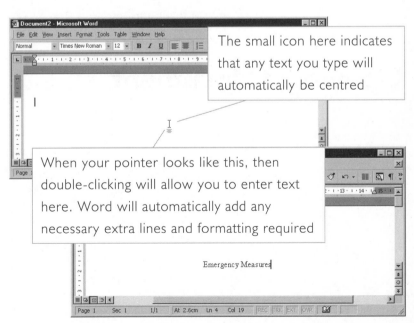

> The small icon here indicates that any text you type will automatically be centred

> When your pointer looks like this, then double-clicking will allow you to enter text here. Word will automatically add any necessary extra lines and formatting required

Saving a Document

The Save icon

| To Save your work either choose "Save" from the File menu, or click on the Save icon in the toolbar.

The following dialog box will appear:

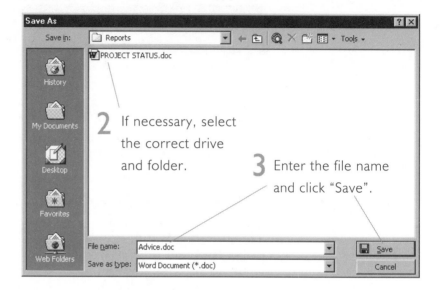

2 If necessary, select the correct drive and folder.

3 Enter the file name and click "Save".

4 If you have finished with the document, choose "Close" from the File menu.

Opening a Document

Either

- Choose "Open" from the File menu or click on the Open icon:

Or

- The last few files used are listed in the lower section of the File menu, and can be selected directly.

Print Preview

The Print Preview icon

Before you print a document, you may wish to check it on screen, in order to eliminate any errors that were not spotted at the basic text-proofing stage. Word 2000 offers a facility, Print Preview, which shows you all the pages of your document exactly as they will print, with none of the modifications made by the normal Word views. To access this special view, select "Print Preview" from the File menu, or select the corresponding icon from the Toolbar.

The following screen appears:

To edit the text in Print Preview, click here – the cursor changes back to its normal text-editing shape – then click in the text and make your changes.

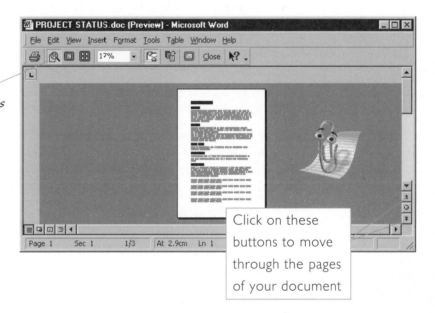

Click on these buttons to move through the pages of your document

Note that the cursor is initially in the shape of a magnifying glass. To zoom in to a particular area of the page, click over it with the left Mouse button; to zoom out, do the same.

If you are satisfied with your document, select "Print" from the File menu, or click the Print icon: 🖨 (see the following page). If you want to continue editing it, click "Close" instead.

Printing a Document

│ Choose "Print" from the File menu.

The following dialog box will appear:

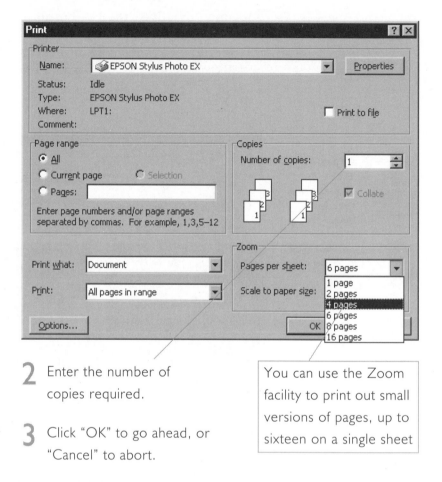

2 Enter the number of
copies required.

3 Click "OK" to go ahead, or
"Cancel" to abort.

You can use the Zoom
facility to print out small
versions of pages, up to
sixteen on a single sheet

The above method allows you the greatest control over how
your document is printed. If, however, you do not need to
make refinements to the printing method, there is a much
quicker way to print: simply click the Toolbar Print icon:

This begins to print immediately, bypassing the Print dialog
box and using the default print settings.

Formatting Text

This chapter looks at ways in which you can change the appearance of your text. We'll start by examining what we can change on a character level. Then we'll see what we can control on a paragraph by paragraph basis.

Covers

Chapter Three

Character-level Formatting

What does "Character-level" mean?

Character-level attributes include font name, size, emboldening, underlining plus all sorts of other effects which can be applied to individual characters. If required, every single character could be given different attributes (although this would tend to make your document look a little like a ransom letter).

Using the Formatting Toolbar

1 Select the text which you want to format.

2 Choose the font required from the pop-up menu in the toolbar:

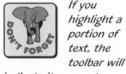

If you highlight a portion of text, the toolbar will indicate its current formatting options.

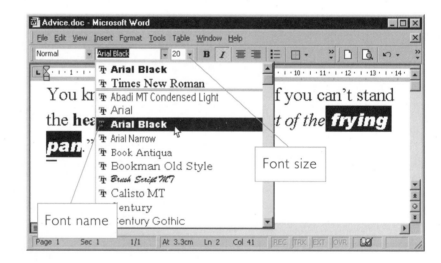

A font is a collection of characters with a particular visual style. Common fonts include:

Times or Times New Roman (useful for main text)

Arial (useful for headings)

Courier (the typewriter font)

3 Look at the font names in the pop-up list:

Printer icon

The most recently used fonts
appear above this line.

TrueType symbol

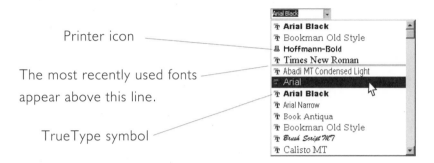

- A printer icon beside the name indicates a printer font. Your machine will use the closest available screen font (which may not match the printed output exactly).

- A double T symbol indicates a TrueType font, which is used for both screen display and printing.

- No symbol beside the font name indicates a screen font. Always check that your printer can reproduce this to a high enough quality.

4 You can use the buttons on this toolbar to add effects such as Bold, Italic, and Underline:

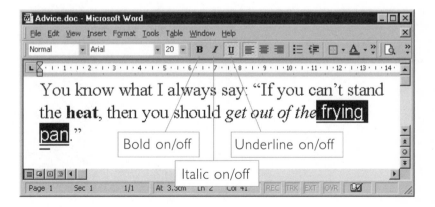

The Font Dialog Box

This controls all aspects of character-level formatting.

1 Select the text to change.

2 Either choose "Font" from the Format menu, then go to step 4, or click your right Mouse button inside the document window.

Right-clicking brings up a pop-up menu that contains options which are relevant to the task in hand. Later you will see that it changes depending on your current context.

To change font quickly, press Control+Shift+F then type the first few letters of the Font name.

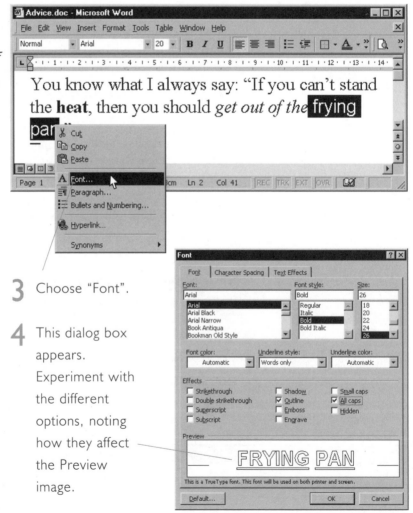

3 Choose "Font".

4 This dialog box appears. Experiment with the different options, noting how they affect the Preview image.

5 Click on the Character Spacing tab.

From here you can numerically control the character spacing, the position (for superscript and subscript), and kerning.

Kerning is a process used to adjust the space between certain combinations of characters. For example, when the letters "T" and "o" occur next to each other, normal spacing appears to be too wide. Kerning brings these together to create the illusion of normal spacing. Since kerning slows down the computer you can either switch it off altogether or activate it only for larger font sizes (where space is more noticeable).

6 Click on the Text Effects tab.

This feature allows you to enhance text by adding animated effects to it. Until a printer manufacturer manages to develop moving ink, these effects will only be visible in on-line documents.

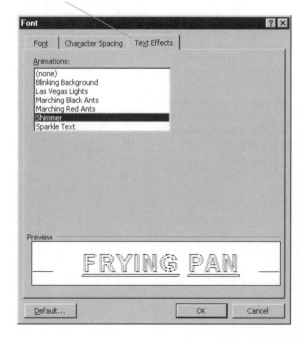

Paragraph-level Formatting

What does "Paragraph-level" mean?

Options such as alignment, left and right indents, and space above and below refer to whole paragraphs, i.e. each paragraph has only one set of these attributes.

Formatting with the Toolbar

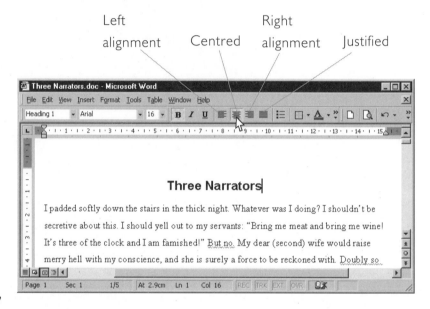

Left alignment   Centred   Right alignment   Justified

If you are changing just one paragraph you need only click an insertion point somewhere within it. Any change to a paragraph-level attribute will always affect the entire paragraph surrounding the insertion point.

I   Select the paragraph(s) to format. Remember that a heading is often a single-line paragraph.

2   Choose the form of alignment by clicking on the appropriate tool in the formatting toolbar.

Forms of Alignment

There are four forms of alignment:

Left
Text lines up along its left edge, with a ragged right edge.

Right
Here the text is moved so that the right edge is straight, and the left is ragged.

Center
Text is centred between the left and right edges.

Justification
The text spacing is adjusted so that each line within a paragraph begins and ends in the same position (dictated by the margins and indents), giving a neat and regular appearance. Below is an example of justified text:

The last line of every justified paragraph is only aligned left, allowing the reader to easily distinguish one paragraph from another.

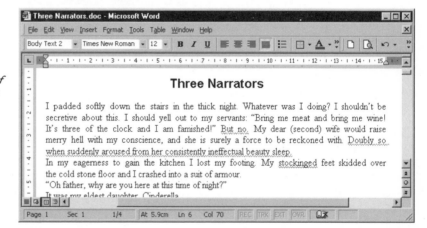

Bulleted Paragraphs

Activating Bullets

1 Select the paragraphs to be bulleted.

2 Click on the Bullet icon in the Formatting toolbar…

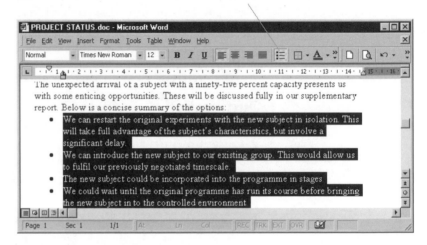

Removing Bullets

1 If necessary, re-select the bulleted paragraphs.

2 Click on the Bullet icon a second time.

Automatic Bullets

This is similar to the automatic numbering feature discussed on page 41. If you begin a paragraph with an asterisk, enter text in the normal way, and then press Return – Word 2000 automatically replaces the asterisk with a bullet, and starts the next paragraph with another. When you reach the end of the list that you want bulleted, erase the bullet that has just been created.

Advanced Bulleting

1 Select the text to be bulleted.

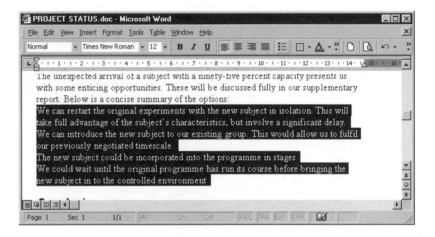

2 Choose "Bullets and Numbering" from the Format menu.

If necessary, click on the "Bulleted" tab.

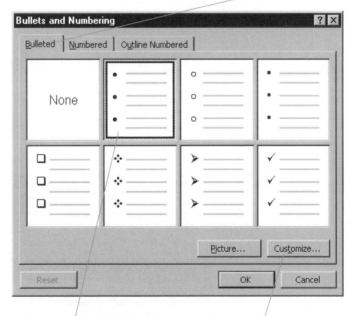

3 Choose the type of bullet text.

4 Click on "Customize" to see further options.

The following dialog box appears:

5 Choose the required settings. Click on the required bullet...

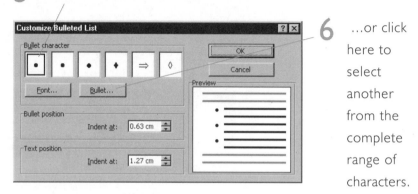

6 ...or click here to select another from the complete range of characters.

7 Select the font and character.

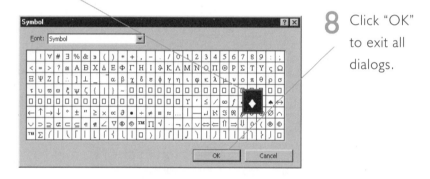

8 Click "OK" to exit all dialogs.

The selected text is now bulleted:

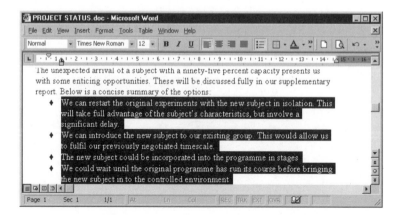

Numbered Paragraphs

1 Select the paragraphs to be numbered.

2 Click on the Numbering icon in the Formatting toolbar:

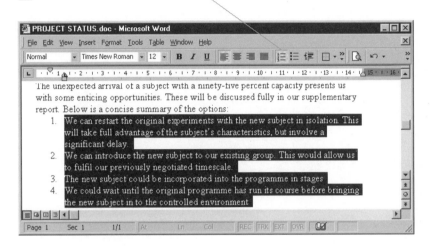

Removing Numbers

1 If necessary, re-select the numbered paragraphs.

2 Click on the Numbering icon a second time.

Automatic Numbering

If you begin a paragraph with a number, enter text in the normal way, and then press Return – Word 2000 automatically starts the next paragraph with the next number. When you reach the end of the list that you want numbered, simply erase the number that has just been created.

Advanced Numbering

1 Select the text to be numbered.

2 Right-click on the selected text, then choose "Bullets and Numbering" from the pop-up menu.

3 Select the "Numbered" tab.

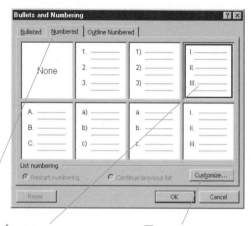

4 Choose a style.

5 Click on "Customize".

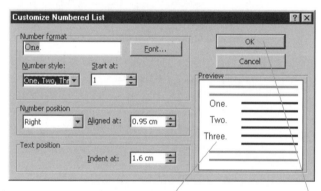

6 Experiment with different settings, referring to the Preview box.

7 Click "OK" to exit all dialog boxes.

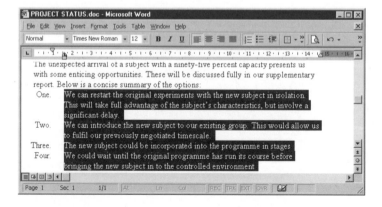

Outline Numbered Lists

Outline numbered lists contain nested sets of headings and subheadings. Because this function helps you to structure your numbered lists, you are likely to use it differently to the normal numbering function (discussed on the previous page).

With the cursor positioned at the point where you want to begin your multi-level structured list, select "Bullets and Numbering" from the Format menu, and choose the Outline Numbered tab.

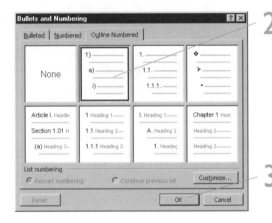

2 Select one of the numbering styles from the top row (i.e., those that don't contain any heading styles).

3 Click OK.

4 In the Word document, enter your list, pressing Return at the end of each element (now see the HOT TIP in the margin).

To place a line at a subordinate level to the one above it, right-click anywhere in the line, and select "Increase Indent". To move a line to a higher level, select "Decrease Indent".

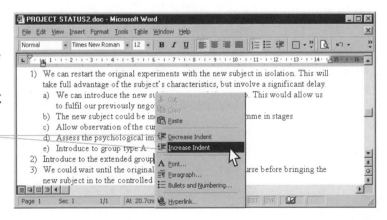

The Paragraph Dialog Box

This controls all aspects of paragraph-level formatting.

1 Select the text to be formatted.

2 Either choose "Paragraph" from the Format menu, or...

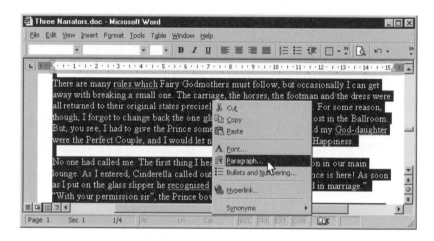

3 ...click your right Mouse button somewhere within the document window and select "Paragraph" from the pop-up menu.

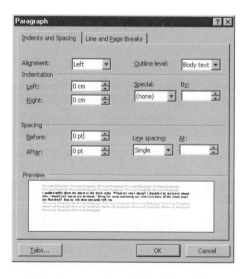

4 Experiment with the different paragraph controls, checking the results in the preview image. You can adjust the left and right indent, the space above and below a paragraph, or the line spacing within a paragraph.

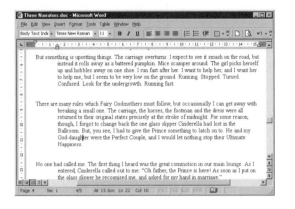

Here, a (vertical) "space before" of 6 points and a special hanging indent of 1.5cm have been set

"Hanging indent" keeps the first line of each paragraph at the left margin, while moving all subsequent lines to the right by a fixed distance.

In the following example, the line spacing has been changed to "exactly" 16 points. This means that each line in the selected paragraphs will be given exactly 16 points of vertical space regardless of the size of font.

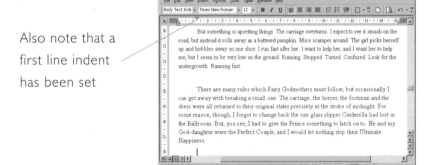

Also note that a first line indent has been set

The Points System of Measurement

This system was introduced firstly in the USA in the nineteenth century, and then adopted by the UK and some European countries.

72 points are equal to 1 inch. 12 points are equal to the size of normal typewriter text.

It provides a standard way of measuring the size of type, and often refers to the vertical dimension of characters in a given font. For this reason it is often useful to adjust vertical spacing using points, so that the space between paragraphs uses the same measuring system as the paragraphs themselves.

The Line and Page Breaks Tab

1 Activate the Paragraph dialog box (either from the Format menu or by clicking in the document window with the right Mouse button).

2 Choose the Line and Page Breaks tab.

A widow is a single line of text at the beginning of a paragraph separated from the rest by a page break. An orphan is a similar line at the end of a paragraph.

Both widows and orphans look unattractive and should be avoided wherever possible.

Instructs Word to automatically move text onto the next page if necessary to prevent widows and orphans occurring

Makes sure that the text is kept with the following paragraph, and not broken over two pages

Word will move the text so that the paragraph is not broken over two pages

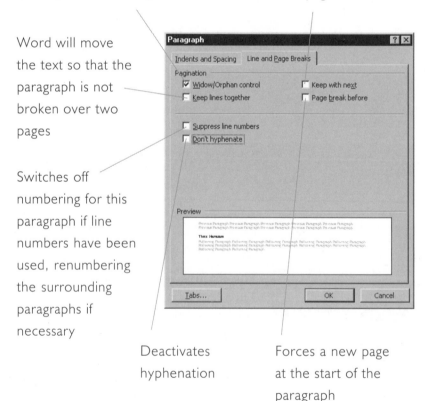

Switches off numbering for this paragraph if line numbers have been used, renumbering the surrounding paragraphs if necessary

Deactivates hyphenation

Forces a new page at the start of the paragraph

Working with a Document

This chapter helps you to find your way around a document, looking at scrolling, selecting different views and zooming in and out of the page. Additionally we'll look at Cut, Copy and Paste, the Format Painter tool and several other helpful document-formatting features.

Covers

Chapter Four

Scrolling

The scroll boxes let you know where you are in a document. For example, when the vertical scroll box is right at the top of the scroll bar, you are looking at the top (the beginning) of the document.

When your text is too large for the document window, you'll need to use one of the following navigation methods:

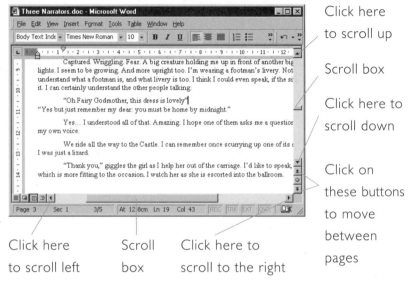

Click here to scroll up

Scroll box

Click here to scroll down

Click on these buttons to move between pages

Click here to scroll left

Scroll box

Click here to scroll to the right

As you scroll down, the scroll box moves down like a lift through a lift shaft. The size of the box indicates how much of the document you are currently viewing. For example, if the box is one third the size of the scroll bar, then you're viewing a third of the document.

Quick Ways to Scroll

- Drag the scroll box directly to a new position.

- Click in the scroll bar to either side of the scroll box. The document will scroll in that direction one screen at a time.

- As you move your insertion point, Word will scroll automatically so that it can always be seen.

The Page Up and Page Down keys will scroll up and down one screen at a time.

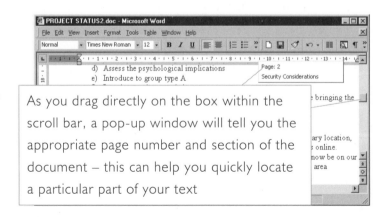

As you drag directly on the box within the scroll bar, a pop-up window will tell you the appropriate page number and section of the document – this can help you quickly locate a particular part of your text

Zooming

You can use the Zoom pop-up menu to control the level of magnification used by the document window.

Either choose an option from the pop-up menu or enter a new percentage value between 10 and 500.

If you can afford the space on screen, always maximise both the document window and the Word window itself by clicking on the Maximise button.

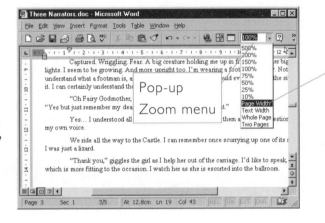

The Page Width option automatically zooms in or out so that the entire width of the page is displayed

In Print Layout view there are options to display one or more entire pages at a time.

Remember that the more you magnify the page, the more you'll need to scroll. Always try to view the entire horizontal line of text, since frequent horizontal scrolling can be tedious.

Resizing Windows

To allocate the greatest possible amount of space to a window, click on the Maximise button. To restore it to its non-maximised size, click on the Restore button.

The Restore symbol indicates that a window is already maximised. Click on this to restore the window to its normal size.

 Maximise button   Restore button

These are located in a window's top right-hand corner. To adjust the dimensions of a non-maximised window, rest the cursor over one of the window's edges (the cursor changes to a double-headed arrow), then drag the edge to where you want it.

The Ruler

The ruler gives you a visual account of the tabs and indents used for any selected text.

1 If the ruler is not visible, activate it by choosing "Ruler" from the View menu.

2 Select one or more paragraphs of text. Experiment by moving the indent markers:

General
left indent
marker

First-line
indent
marker

Default
tab stops

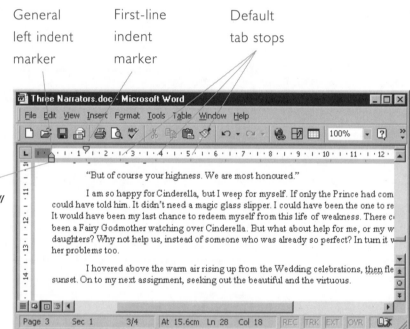

There is a small square block directly below the left indent marker.
Dragging this will move both the left and first line indent markers together.

The Paragraph Dialog Box
You can also access these controls numerically from the Paragraph dialog box. See "The Paragraph Dialog Box" on page 44.

Cut and Paste

1 Select the text to be moved.

2 Right-click on the selected text, then choose "Cut".

You can also Cut and Paste using the Edit menu, or the keyboard shortcuts Control+X and Control+V respectively.

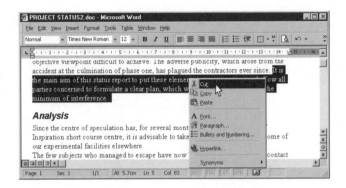

The text is removed and put into the Clipboard.

3 Next position the insertion point at the destination. Click the right Mouse button, then choose "Paste".

You can also make use of the Cut, Copy and Paste buttons in the Standard Toolbar:

 Cut

 Copy

 Paste

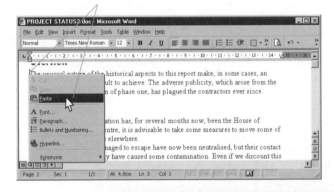

The text is pasted here

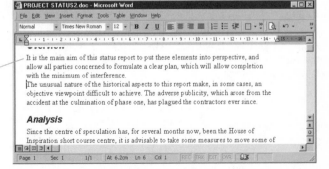

Copy and Paste

1 Select the text to be copied.

2 Right-click on the selected text, then choose "Copy".

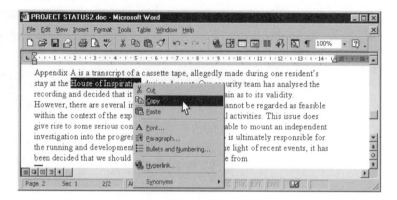

The quickest way to move text is to select it, then drag (from anywhere within the selected area) directly to the new position.

The text is copied into the Clipboard.

3 Next, position the insertion point at the destination. Click the right Mouse button, then choose "Paste".

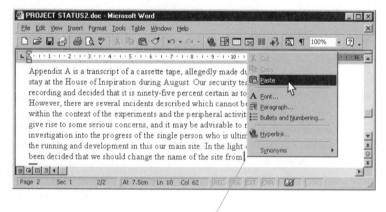

If you drag the selected area with the Control key held down, then the text will be copied to the new position.

The copied text will paste here

Once something is in the Clipboard, you can paste it as many times as you like.

Collect and Paste

Word 2000 can also make use of a special Clipboard toolbar. This allows you to store more than one item in the Clipboard.

I Open the View menu and choose "Toolbars". Make sure that the Clipboard toolbar is active.

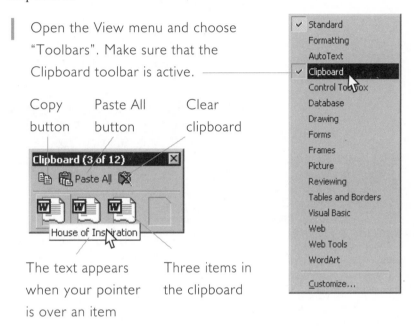

Copy button

Paste All button

Clear clipboard

The text appears when your pointer is over an item

Three items in the clipboard

2 Each time you choose Copy, an extra item appears in the Clipboard. Click where you want to paste an item in your document, then click on the icon in the Clipboard to paste in the contents. Or, click the Paste All button to paste in the whole Clipboard contents.

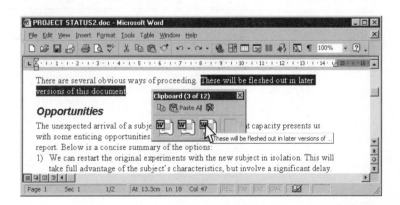

Undo and Redo

- Click the Undo button or type Control+Z to undo the last action.

- Alternatively, open the Undo pop-up menu to review and undo more than one action:

Undo button   Undo drop-down menu button

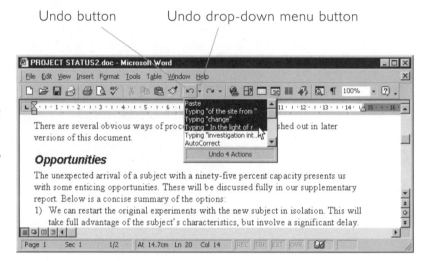

When undoing or redoing actions using the drop-down menus, drag the cursor down until the actions that you want to undo or redo are highlighted, then release the Mouse button.

- To redo the undone actions, type Control+Y or use the Redo pop-up menu.

Redo button   Redo drop-down menu button

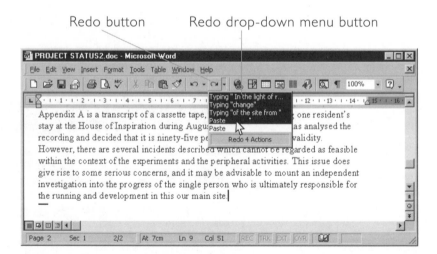

Page Breaks

The keyboard shortcut for page break is Control+Return (or Enter).

To delete a page break, simply select it by clicking in the left margin area and press Delete.

Word automatically calculates the position of page breaks. These appear in the document window as a dotted horizontal line (a "soft" page break). However, you can force page breaks, as follows:

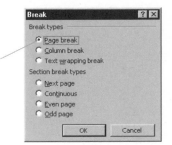

1 Choose "Break..." from the Insert menu.

2 Make sure that "Page break" is selected.

A "Hard" page break is inserted.

Defining Sections

Sections can be used to help organise your document. They also allow you to vary its layout, even within a single page.

1 Click an insertion point part of the way through your document (between paragraphs).

2 Choose "Break" from the Insert menu.

3 Choose the "Continuous" option, under "Section break types".

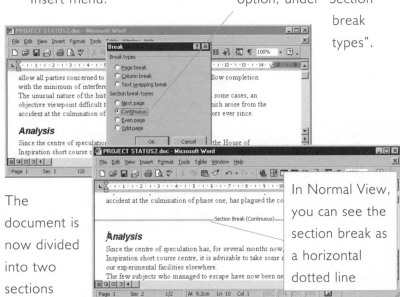

The document is now divided into two sections

In Normal View, you can see the section break as a horizontal dotted line

Using Columns with Sections

1 Make sure you are using a document which has been divided into two or more sections.

2 Click the insertion point somewhere in the second section, then choose "Columns" from the Format menu:

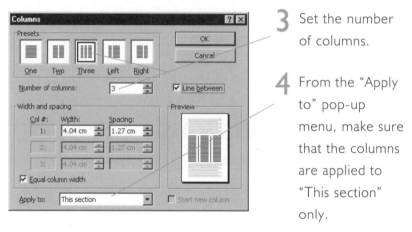

3 Set the number of columns.

4 From the "Apply to" pop-up menu, make sure that the columns are applied to "This section" only.

5 Click "OK".

You now have a mixed column layout:

If you drag with the Alt key held down, Word will display the horizontal measurements in the ruler.

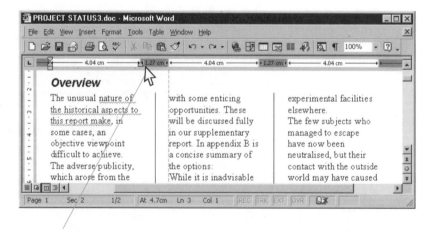

6 You can also adjust the width of columns by dragging the columns' boundary markers in the ruler.

Column Breaks

You can force text to start in a new column by inserting a hard break.

1 Place your insertion point and choose "Break" from the Insert menu.

2 Select the "Column break" radio button, then click OK.

This will force the text after the insertion point into a new column.

Balancing Columns

If there is enough space on the page to accommodate all of your column text, you can balance the columns neatly:

1 Click the insertion point at the end of the last column and choose "Break" from the Insert menu.

2 Insert a "Continuous" section break.

The columns are balanced to within a line or two of each other

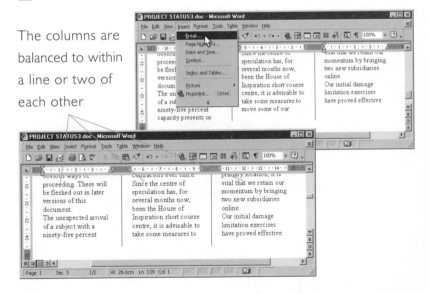

Headers and Footers

Headers normally appear at the top of every page, footers at the bottom (an example being "Word 2000 in easy steps" on this page).

Creating/Modifying a Header

Choose "Header and Footer" from the View menu.

Word will automatically change to Print Layout View. The main page text will be greyed out to let you concentrate on the header. The Header and Footer toolbar will also appear.

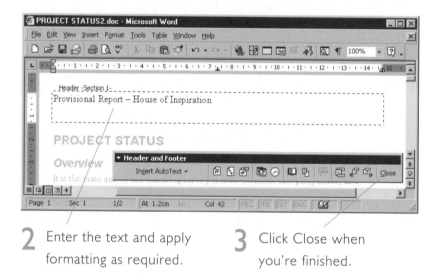

2 Enter the text and apply formatting as required.

3 Click Close when you're finished.

The Header and Footer Toolbar

Switch between header and footer

Insert page number

Format page number

Insert date

Page setup

Same as previous

Show previous

Show next

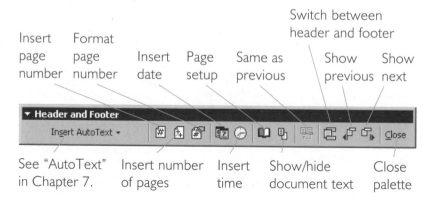

See "AutoText" in Chapter 7.

Insert number of pages

Insert time

Show/hide document text

Close palette

Creating/Modifying a Footer

1 Click on the "Switch between header and footer" button in the toolbar. This will take you to the footer text.

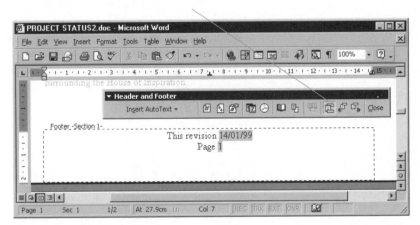

2 Enter the footer text. You can include automatic page numbers, or the current date or time by clicking on the relevant button in the toolbar.

3 Click "Close" when you've finished.

By default, the header and footer on a page will apply to all remaining pages in the document. You can override this by editing the headers/footers for other pages separately.

Now the header and footer text is greyed out, and you can edit the main text again. Note that the picture below shows Print Layout View. In Normal View, headers and footers do not appear at all.

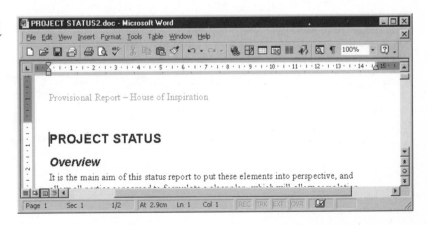

The Format Painter

This allows you to copy the formatting options from one piece of text to another:

1 Select the source text and click on the Format Painter icon.

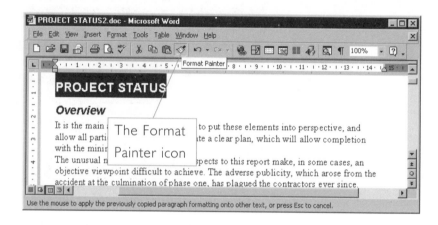

The Format Painter icon

2 Now drag across the destination text. The formatting is applied to the new text.

To copy formatting to more than one destination, simply double-click the Format Painter icon. You can then apply the new formatting to as many pieces of text as you wish. When you've finished, either click back on the icon or press the Escape key.

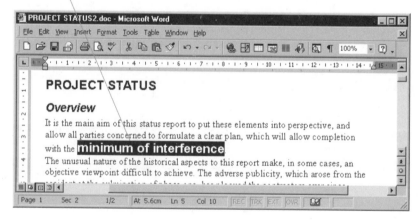

Document Properties

Windows 95/98 (and later versions) allow you to enter file names which are longer (and so more descriptive) than the Spartan eight characters allowed by MS-DOS. Even so, it is useful to record additional information as part of each Word document to help you organise your work, and remember your document's purpose.

1 Go to the File menu and choose "Properties".

2 Enter the relevant details. These will be saved along with your document.

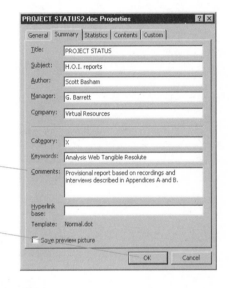

3 Click OK when you're done.

The Statistics tab in the Properties dialog will show you useful information about your document.

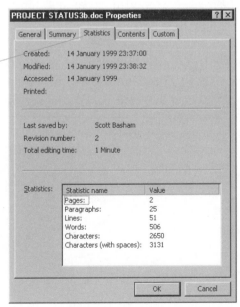

4 When you use the Open document dialog, you can click on the "Advanced" button to tell Word to search on the basis of the information entered in a document's properties.

The Document Map

The Document Map is a feature new to Word 2000, which uses the headings in your document to create an outline of the document's structure. It appears in a separate pane to the left of the main editing area, and can be used to navigate easily through the document. To display the Document Map, do the following:

| Click on the Document Map button.

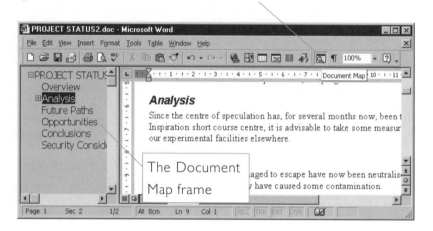

The Document Map frame

2 To jump to a heading listed in the Document Map, simply click on its entry.

Note that, in the illustration above, the heading "Analysis" has a small plus-sign next to it. This indicates that there are subheadings beneath it. To display these headings, click on the plus sign:

To collapse the structure to show only the main headings, click on the minus-sign

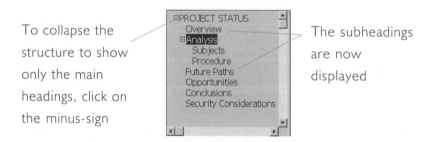

The subheadings are now displayed

Styles and Themes

Styles help you to easily apply a consistent set of formatting commands to main text, headings and other elements of your document.

Once you start using styles, you'll be able to control your document's presentation with the minimum of tedious manual editing.

Themes allow you to give a collection of your documents the same consistent look and feel.

Covers

Chapter Five

Using the Default Styles

A style is a complete collection of type attributes saved under a single name. There are two main benefits to this:

- Your document will have a visual consistency if, for example, all your subheadings look the same.

- You can quickly make drastic but coherent changes to the format of your document by redefining the styles already used by the text.

Applying a Style

I Select the text.

2 Select a style from the Style drop-down menu:

You can also use the keyboard shortcut Control+Shift+S to activate the Style button. Then type the first few letters of the style, press the down arrow key, and press Return to apply the style.

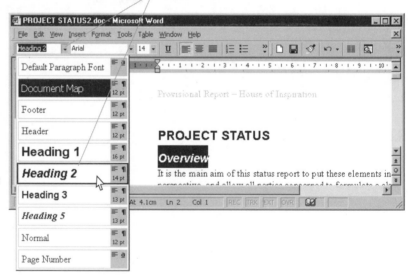

The text has now been set to this style. Whenever you select text on the page, the Style menu will indicate which style is currently being used.

By default all text starts off using the style "Normal".

Editing an Existing Style

1 Select some text in the document which already uses the style to be changed.

2 Use the toolbar and menus as normal to experiment with changes in formatting (see Chapter Three).

3 When you are happy with the changes, reselect the style from the pop-up list:

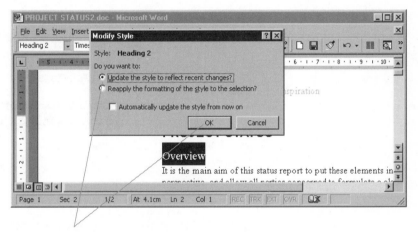

4 In the dialog which appears, make sure the "Update the style..." option is selected and click "OK".

All text in the document using this style will now change automatically...

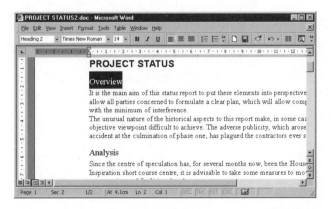

Creating a New Style

You can easily create a new text style in Word 2000, simply by altering existing text, and then entering a name for the new style, which will take these properties.

1 Format the text as normal in the document (see Chapter Three), then select it.

2 When you are happy with its appearance, click on the Style menu box, enter the new style's name, and press Enter:

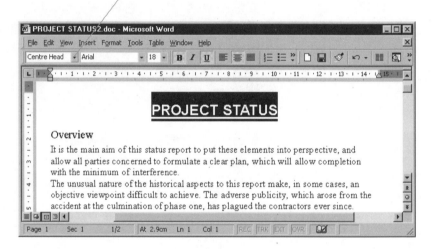

The new style is automatically created, and can now be applied to other text.

Automatic Style Creation

When you alter the formatting of text, Word 2000 can create a new style for you. For example, if you enter a small number of words without punctuation on a single line, apply some changes to the font, size or font effects, and then press Enter, Word will usually assume that this is a new heading style, and create a new style automatically. Thus, if you already have three heading styles, named "Heading 1", "Heading 2", etc., the new style will be named "Heading 4".

The Style Dialog Box

Word 2000 allows you to make most of the style changes you should need from the Formatting toolbar; but the Style dialog allows you to preview potential style changes on a large portion of text, and then to cancel out of the dialog without actually making any of the changes. To open the dialog, do the following:

Select "Style" from the Format menu. The dialog appears:

Creating a New Style Using the Style Dialog Box

1 Click on the "New" button in the Style dialog box (see above).

2 Enter the new style's name.

3 See the "Setting the Format" topic on the following page to see how to change the new style's properties.

Setting the Format

1 Click on the Format button in the New Style dialog box:

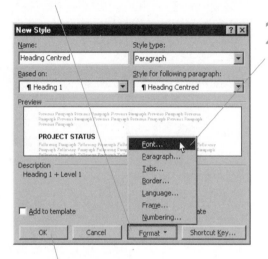

2 This menu appears, from which you can select the dialogs that control the various properties of the style. Make the appropriate changes, referring to the formatting topics in Chapters 2, 3 and 4.

3 When you have made your changes, click "OK". The new style is added to the list.

Modifying a Style

1 From the Styles dialog box, click on "Modify".

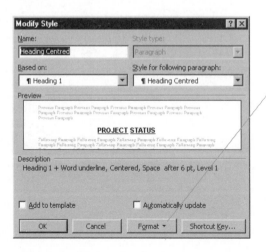

2 Use the Format button to make the desired changes (see "Setting the Format", step 2, above), then click "OK".

Setting a Keyboard Shortcut for a Style

1 Click the "Shortcut Key" button in the Modify Style or New Style dialog box.

The Customize Keyboard dialog appears:

Word tells you if your proposed shortcut key is currently being used for something else. If you go ahead, then your style shortcut will override the previous setting.

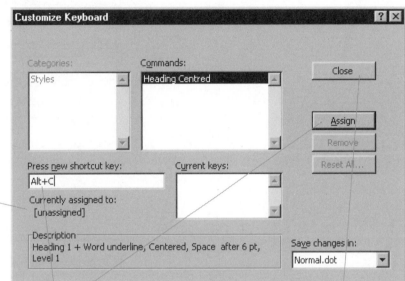

Most single keystrokes will already be assigned a function, so you will probably need to use a combination of keys, using the Ctrl and/or Alt keys. When you enter the shortcut key combination, all you have to do is press the keys that you want to use: you don't have to type out "Ctrl" or "Alt" in full.

2 Enter the shortcut key combination for the style and click the "Assign" button. You can repeat this process to add more than one keyboard shortcut for the same style.

3 When you have finished, click the "Close" button to return to the previous dialog box.

Character-level Styles

Normally styles operate on a paragraph level, i.e. they only apply to whole paragraphs.

To create a character-level style:

1 Choose "New" from the Style dialog.

2 Select "Character" from the "Style type" pop-up menu.

3 Enter a name for the new style here.

4 Use the "Format" pop-up to set the character-level attributes.

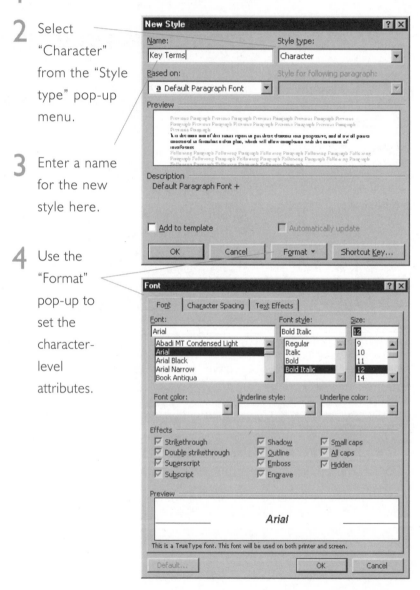

You can now apply your character style to individual words or phrases without affecting the entire surrounding paragraph.

If text already uses a paragraph style, then the character style will override these settings:

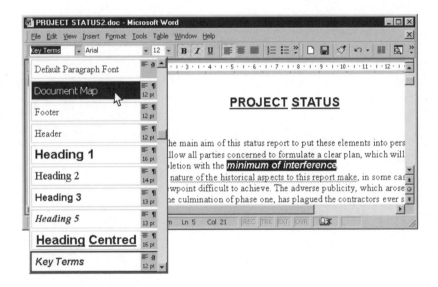

Identifying Character and Paragraph Style Names

Character-level style names are labelled in the pop-up list with **a**. Paragraph styles are labelled with ¶.

Once a style has been created, it cannot be changed from a character to a paragraph style, or vice versa. However, you can always create a new copy of the style by choosing "Styles" from the Format menu, then selecting the style you want to copy and then clicking on "New". Since this is a new style you can now select the style type.

AutoFormat

Word uses a feature called AutoFormat to apply suitable styles automatically to the different parts of your document, without you having to select them. For example, it analyses whether a paragraph seems to be functioning as body text, as a heading, or as part of a list. AutoFormat is turned on by default, but you can change this as follows:

1. Choose "AutoCorrect" from the Tools menu, then select the "AutoFormat As You Type" tab.

2. Select which formatting changes AutoFormat should make automatically as you enter your text.

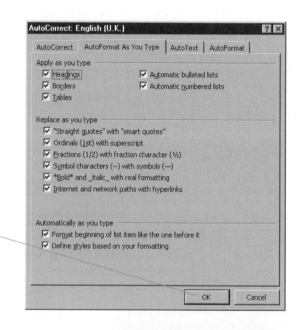

3. Click "OK".

If AutoFormat has been deactivated while you have typed in a document, and you subsequently want to have the document formatted automatically, do the following:

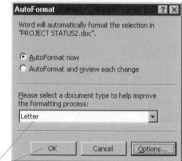

1. Select "AutoFormat" from the Format menu.

2. Tell Word what sort of document this is, then click "OK".

Themes

Themes allow you to give a unified look and feel to a document. They contain settings for styles, bullets, colour and graphics.

Applying a Theme to a Document

If you have Microsoft FrontPage version 4 (or later) installed, you can use its Themes as well as those supplied with Word.

You can also download additional Themes by choosing "Microsoft on the Web" from the Help menu.

1 Choose "Theme" from the Format menu. The following dialog box appears:

2 Select a Theme from the list.

3 Check the sample of the theme. If you are happy with its look, then click "OK".

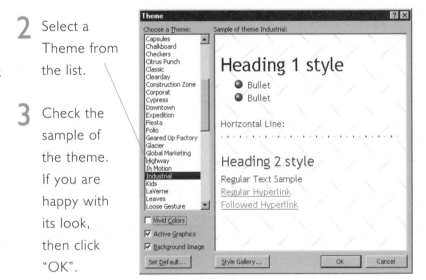

Your document will now reflect the new Theme.

You can still change your mind at this point by using the Undo button.

Alternatively, select a different Theme from the Theme dialog box.

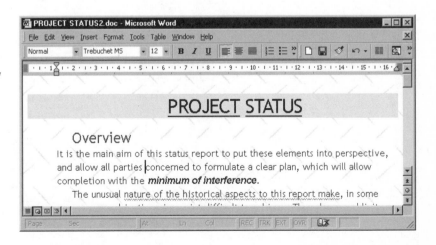

The Style Gallery

When you work on a document, a template is used to tell Word which formatting properties to use for the different character and paragraph styles. You can use the Style Gallery to apply the properties of different templates, to produce an instant overall change to the appearance of your document.

A Template differs from a Theme in that it only contains style definit-ions, and no colour schemes or graphics. However, a Template will generally contain far more style definitions than a Theme.

1 Go to the Format menu, and choose "Theme".

2 Click on the Style Gallery button.

3 Choose a template design, then a preview option.

"Document" shows you how your document would look with the proposed style definitions. "Example" shows you an example document, demonstrating the different styles.

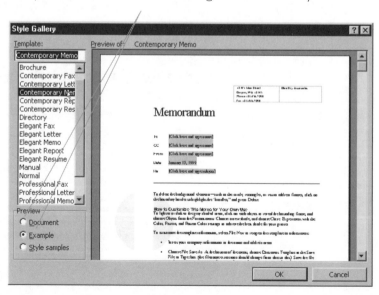

"Style samples" lists each style name using its own attributes

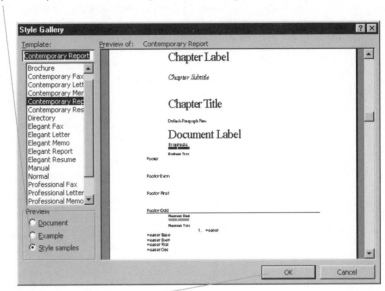

4 Click "OK" if you want your document to adopt these new style definitions.

Your document will now use the styles from the template.

If your document currently doesn't use any of the style names defined in the Template, then applying the Template will have no initial visible effect. However, you can now use these new styles by applying them manually to your text.

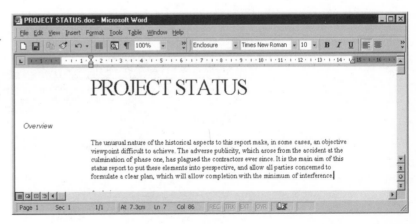

Displaying Style Names

Sometimes it is useful to see instantly which styles are being used by the paragraphs in your document.

1 Make sure that Normal View is active (you can set this using the View menu or the icon at the bottom left of the screen).

2 Choose "Options" from the Tools menu.

3 Click on the View tab.

4 Set the "Style area width" to a figure greater than zero.

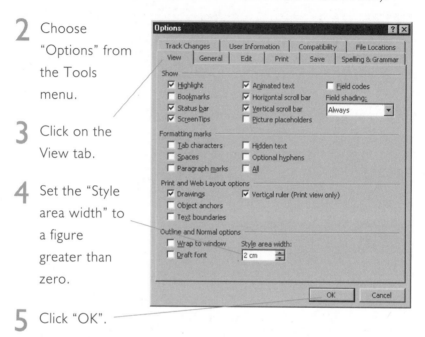

5 Click "OK".

In this example we've used a 2cm margin area in which to list the styles used.

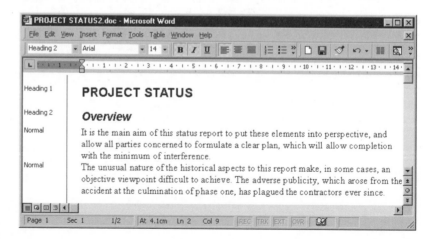

Tabulation

Text which is laid out with correct and accurate horizontal alignment greatly helps to give a document a professional look.

Effective use of white space, including tabulation, is one of the most important considerations when using a word-processor. This chapter deals with a range of tabulation features and examples.

Covers

Chapter Six

Default Tabulation

The default tab stops are set every half inch. When you press the Tab key, Word automatically moves across the page, stopping when it reaches the next tab stop position.

To see how this works:

1 Make sure that the ¶ button is active.

2 Enter items of text separated by a single tab character.

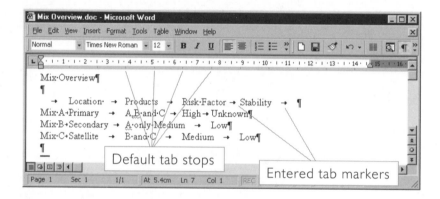

Default tab stops

Entered tab markers

Creating Your Own Tabulation

1 Select the text.

2 Click in the lower half of the ruler (or the grey bar beneath it) to create a new tab (shaped like an "L") and drag to adjust its position.

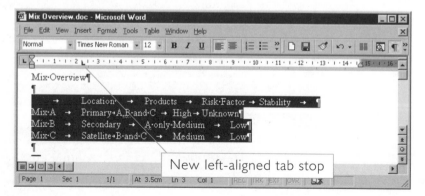

New left-aligned tab stop

Any new tab stops you create will automatically override the default tabs.

3 Repeat this process to create more tab stops.

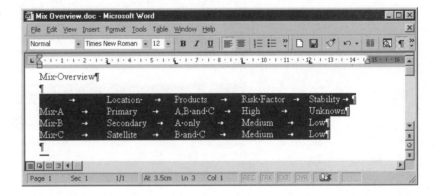

Deleting Tabs

You can delete your tab stops simply by dragging them downwards out of the ruler.

Different Types of Tab

You can move your own tab stops at any time by dragging them within the ruler – but be sure to select the main text first.

So far you've created left-aligned tabs, which cause text to align along its left edge under the tab stop.

1 Click the Tab Alignment button once to change to centre tabs.

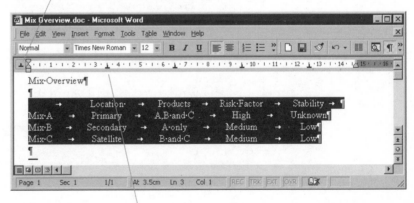

2 You can now create centred tabs by clicking in the ruler.

As you click on the Tab Alignment button, it cycles between Left, Centre, Right and Decimal alignment.

Here is an example of right-aligned tabs:

Tabulation is a paragraph-level attribute. Each paragraph can have its own tab stops if necessary.

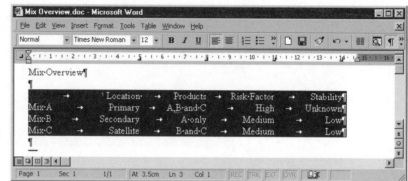

Decimal tabs are used to line up numbers along the decimal point:

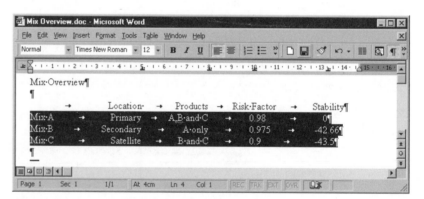

Usually a mixture of different tabs is required:

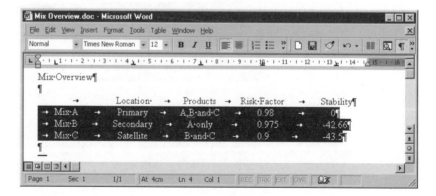

The Tabs Dialog Box

More options can be found in the Tabs dialog box.

You can also access the Tabs dialog box by double-clicking directly on a Tab marker in the Ruler.

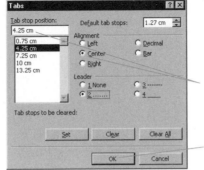

1 Choose "Tabs" from the Format menu.

2 Set the position and alignment of the tab.

3 Click "OK".

This example also uses a leader consisting of a row of dots

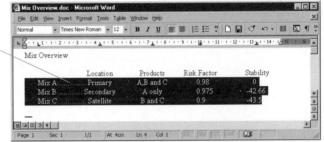

Bar Tabs

These can only be accessed from the Tabs dialog box (follow the steps above). Setting a bar tab causes a vertical line to appear in the text at the specified position.

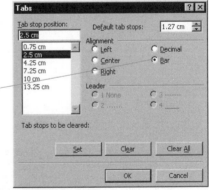

You can also access the Tabs dialog via the Paragraph dialog (see
page 44).

Bar tab

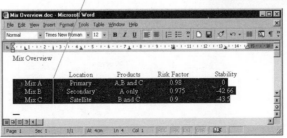

Using Tabs to Create Tables

The examples used on the preceding pages of this chapter have demonstrated the properties of tabs by using them to create a simple table. However, although this table presents a small amount of information clearly, it contains none of the additional effects that are often used to enhance the presentation of tables: e.g., borders, shaded cells. Word 2000 does allow you to create tables that can use such effects, using a very simple click-and-drag method (see Chapter 10, "Tables and Charts", for how to do this); but if you have already entered your table data as we have in this chapter, you won't want to type it in all over again. Fortunately, Word allows you to convert such data into true tables very easily:

1 Highlight the data you want to convert.

2 Go to the Table menu, open the Convert submenu and choose "Text to Table".

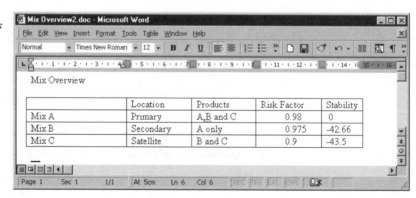

3 If you have separated your columns using tabs, make sure this option is selected.

4 Click "OK". The table is created automatically:

If the width of a column needs adjusting, rest your cursor over the table column icon to its right, then click and drag it to where you want it.

	Location	Products	Risk Factor	Stability
Mix A	Primary	A,B and C	0.98	0
Mix B	Secondary	A only	0.975	-42.66
Mix C	Satellite	B and C	0.9	-43.5

Automatic Features

Word has many automatic features which will operate on selected text or a complete document. This chapter looks at many of these, including search and replace tools and facilities for correction of spelling and grammar.

Covers

Chapter Seven

Find and Replace

Finding Text

Word can be instructed to search through your document for particular words, groups of characters, or formatting attributes.

1 Choose "Find" from the Edit menu, or type Control+F.

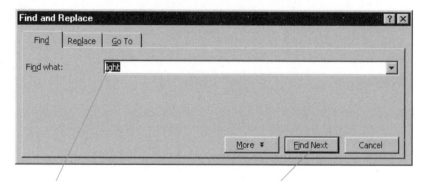

2 Enter your search text here.

3 Click on the Find Next button.

Word keeps this dialog box open in case you want to search on to the next occurrence of your text.

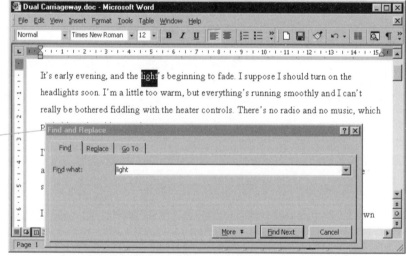

Word will highlight the next instance of the search text within your document. The Office Assistant will let you know if the end of the document was reached without Word finding any occurrences.

Even if you close the Find and Replace dialog, you can still continue your search by using the two blue buttons in the vertical scrollbar.

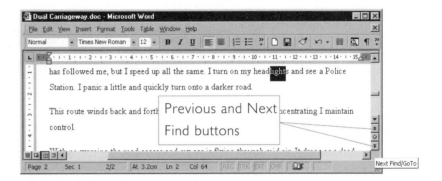

More or Less

1 If the Find and Replace dialog is not currently being displayed, then choose "Find" from the Edit menu, or type Control+F.

2 Click the More button to display more options, or the Less button to see the abbreviated version of this dialog box.

Using the checkboxes in the centre of the dialog, you can set the Find dialog to look for text in a particular case, for whole words (rather than groups of letters), to use wildcard searching, or phonetic matching.

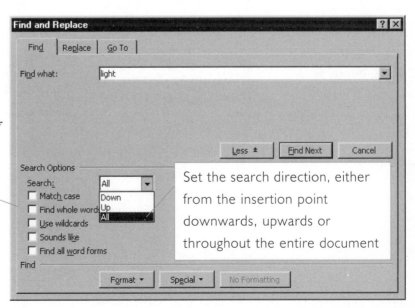

Searches based on Attributes

Your search can be based on attributes as well as specific text. You can even search for particular text and attributes simultaneously.

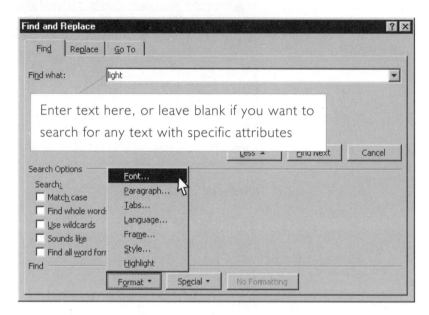

> Enter text here, or leave blank if you want to search for any text with specific attributes

In the Find and Replace dialog box, open the Format pop-up menu and choose the relevant option(s).

In this example we're searching for Arial Italic 11 point text.

2 Click "OK" to return to the Find dialog, then click on the Find button to start the search.

Word will now look through your document to find any text which matches *both* what you typed for "Find what" *and* the attributes you specified:

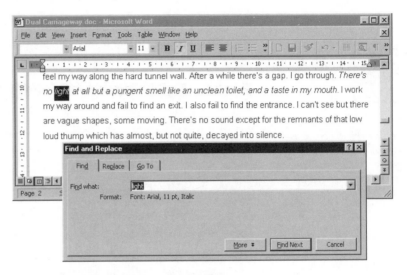

Cancelling Attribute Searches

If you have previously specified attributes for your search, then you can clear these quickly by clicking on the No Formatting button.

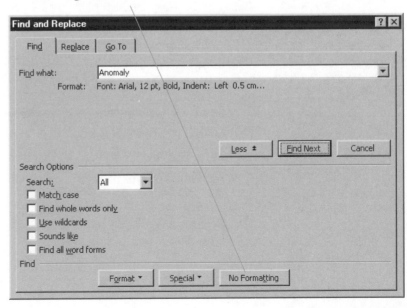

Replacing Text

Once you have found an instance of the text you are searching for, you can choose to replace it with some different text.

Before clicking on the Format button, be sure to click in either the "Find what" or "Replace with" parts of the dialog. This determines whether you want to specify a Format to search for, or to replace with.

| Click on the Replace tab.

2 Enter the "Replace with" text.

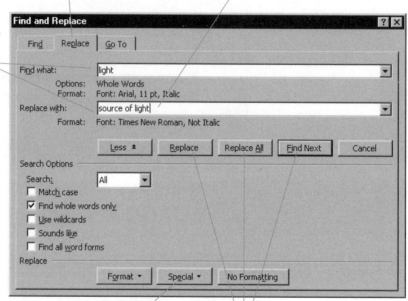

To open the Find and Replace dialog with the Replace tab active, you can choose Replace from the Edit menu, or type Control+H. You can then enter the "Find what" text here before continuing with step 2.

3 If you wish to replace the search text with text that has different format attributes, click here and choose the relevant options.

4 Click "Replace" to change just this instance of the target text, "Replace All" to change every instance in the document, or "Find Next" to skip to the next instance.

5 When you're done, click "Cancel".

Special Characters

You can use the "Special" pop-up menu in the Find and Replace tabs to easily insert the keyboard codes for special characters.

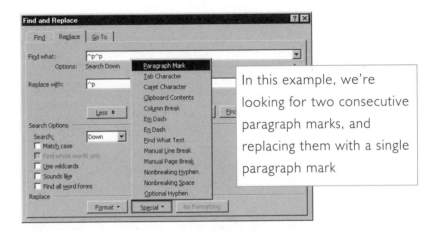

In this example, we're looking for two consecutive paragraph marks, and replacing them with a single paragraph mark

Wildcards

If you want to search not for a specific piece of text, but for text that follows a certain pattern, select the "Use wildcards" checkbox before clicking the "Special" button. You will then find that "Special" pop-up menu contains some extra entries – e.g. to search for words that follow the pattern "g?ve" (where "?" represents any single character), you would do the following:

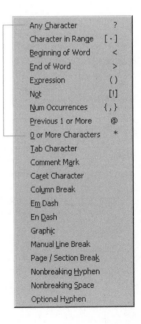

1. Enter the letter "g" in the "Find what" box.

2. Click the "Special" button and select "Any Character" from the menu.

3. Enter the letters "ve".

This search will highlight all words like "give", "gave", and (if you don't have the "Find whole words only" checkbox selected) words like "given", too.

Another very useful wildcard feature available from the "Special" menu is the "Character in Range" function. This allows you to search for numbers or letters in any range you specify. For example, to search for references to years between 1961 and 1967, make sure that the "Use wildcards" checkbox is selected, then do the following:

1 In the "Find what" box, enter "196".

2 Click on the "Special" button and select "Character in Range" from the menu. The text "[-]" will be inserted.

3 Edit the contents of the "Find what" box so that it now reads "196[1-7]".

Spelling and Grammar Checking

The shortcut key for Spelling and Grammar Checking is

F7.

Word allows you to check your spelling and grammar in two ways: either from a special dialog, or "on the fly". The dialog is used as follows.

1 If you don't want to spell check your entire document, then select only the text you require.

2 Choose "Spelling and Grammar" from the Tools menu, or click on the corresponding icon:

Click on Ignore All to skip over all other instances of the current word. Similarly, Change All will apply the current suggestion to all other instances as well.

Word 2000 highlights spelling mistakes in red, and possible grammatical problems in green.

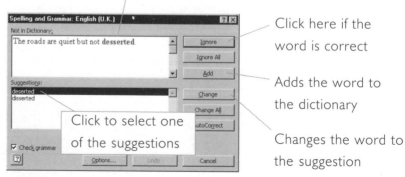

Click here if the word is correct

Adds the word to the dictionary

Changes the word to the suggestion

Click to select one of the suggestions

Here's an example of Word questioning some grammar. The rule being tested is explained by the Office Assistant.

If you disagree with Word's grammar advice, then either click Ignore to skip the current phrase or Ignore Rule to stop Word applying the rule altogether.

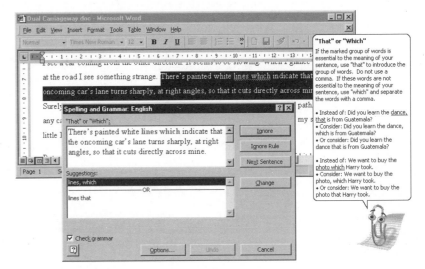

3 Clicking the "Options" button takes you to the "Spelling & Grammar" options dialog box:

You can also access the Spelling & Grammar options as a tab of the main options dialog: select Options from the Tools menu.

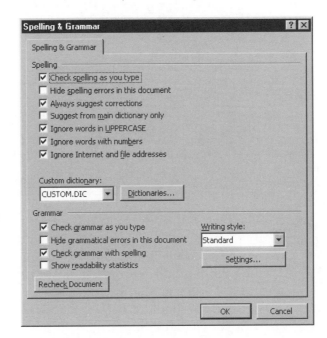

Readability Statistics

It is possible to make Word 2000 display readability statistics for your document, after it has finished performing a Spelling and Grammar check.

1 Select Options from the Tools menu, and choose the Spelling and Grammar tab (illustrated on page 91).

2 Make sure that the "Show readability statistics" checkbox is checked, then click "OK".

After you have performed a Spelling and Grammar check, this dialog is displayed:

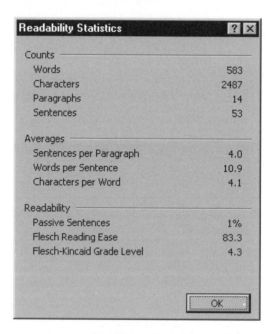

Unfortunately no one has, as yet, figured out a way of automatically analysing the boredom level of a document. This is one job still left to us lucky humans.

A United States Grade Level of 3 roughly equates to an age of 8.

The Flesch Reading Ease value is in the range 0...100, increasing with ease of reading. Standard text rates between 60 and 70. The Grade Level values give an indication as to the school grade appropriate for your text. For example, a level of 3 means that it would be understandable by someone in the third grade or below. Standard text normally weighs in between 7 and 8.

...cont'd

Checking on-the-fly

While the dialog-box method of checking your spelling and grammar offers you the greatest amount of control over exactly how the checking is done, Word 2000 can check your grammar and spelling automatically as you type, highlighting any problems it finds on the page. Consider the following example:

Both the Spelling and the Grammar pop-up menus offer a quick route to the full Spelling and Grammar dialog box. Simply select the bottom entry, marked with:

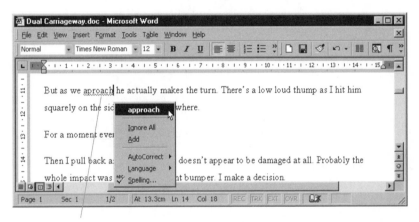

This spelling mistake is underlined in red. To correct, right-click on it then select the correct suggested word from the pop-up menu. If the suggestion is not suitable, attempt to correct it yourself, then see if it is still flagged.

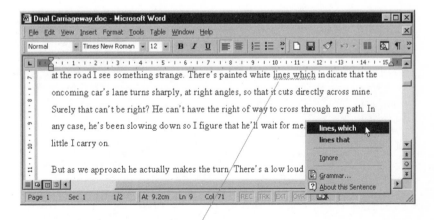

This grammar mistake is underlined in green. Right-click on it, then select the correct suggestion from the menu.

Word Count

Word provides a quick and easy way of counting the number of words in your document:

1 To count the words in one area only, select it in the normal way – otherwise the entire document will be scanned.

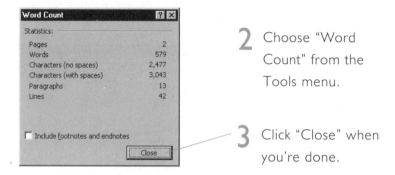

2 Choose "Word Count" from the Tools menu.

3 Click "Close" when you're done.

Thesaurus

If you need to search for a word's synonyms (i.e., words closely related in meaning), you can use the built-in Thesaurus.

1 Select the word to be used.

2 Choose Language>Thesaurus from the Tools menu.

The shortcut to the Thesaurus feature is Shift+F7.

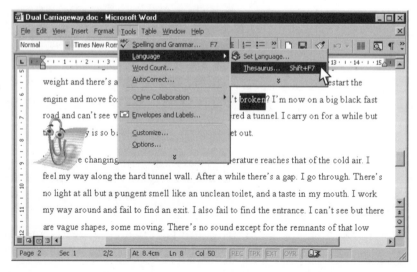

The Thesaurus dialog box appears:

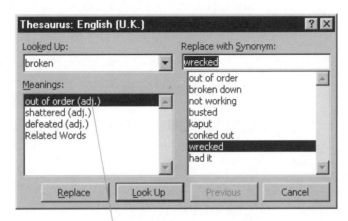

3 Double-click here to search for the related words.

If none of the words you see listed in the Synonyms pane at step 5 are suitable, try clicking on another entry in the Meanings section. Alternatively, double-click on one of the words in the Synonyms area to see the synonyms stored for that word. You can continue in this manner indefinitely.

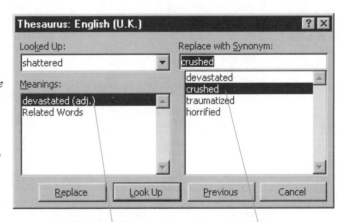

4 The different possible categories of meanings related to your word are listed in this area. Click on whichever best summarises the meaning you are aiming for...

5 ...to see the relevant synonyms listed here. If one of these is suitable, click on it, then click the "Replace" button to change the word in your document.

AutoCorrect

Often, the same spelling or typing mistakes are made again and again. You can instruct Word to substitute the correction automatically :

Choose "AutoCorrect" from the Tools menu, and make sure that this tab is selected.

You don't have to enter all the AutoCorrect data yourself: Word 2000 contains a large number of corrections, including common mistakes for "necessary", "occasion", and transposition errors such as "knwo" instead of "know". You can browse through these from the AutoCorrect dialog.

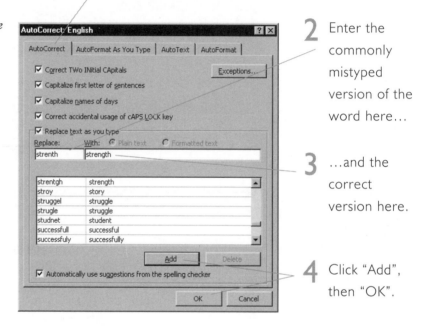

2 Enter the commonly mistyped version of the word here...

3 ...and the correct version here.

4 Click "Add", then "OK".

If you type the error now, Word spots it and substitutes the correct word automatically, instead of merely flagging it as a possible spelling mistake:

| Identified strenths | ... | Identified strengths |

original text typed   *corrected by Word*

You can now continue through the rest of your life completely unaware that you are consistently failing to spell correctly.

AutoText

This is a less automatic version of AutoCorrect, and is useful for setting up your own abbreviations.

If you find that you often need to type the same text, then it would be worth setting up an AutoText entry:

Creating an AutoText Entry

1 Type the text and select it.

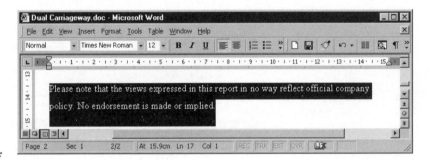

As a shortcut, you can also use the AutoText toolbar button:

If it isn't visible, you can display it by checking the AutoText entry in the View>Toolbars menu.

2 Choose "AutoCorrect" from the Tools menu and select the AutoText tab.

3 Edit the entry in this box to the abbreviation you require.

4 Click "OK".

The selected text is automatically inserted into the this area of the AutoText dialog box.

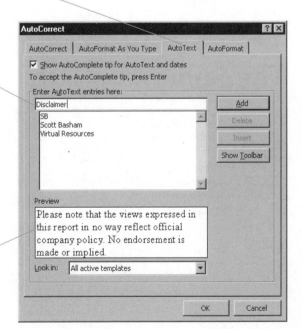

Using AutoText

You can also insert AutoText by selecting it from the AutoText tab of the Tools> AutoCorrect dialog box.

1 Simply type the abbreviation:

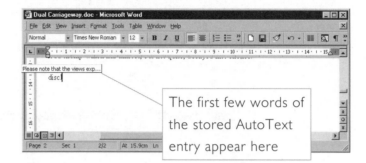

The first few words of the stored AutoText entry appear here

2 Press Enter or F3 to replace the abbreviation with the full text.

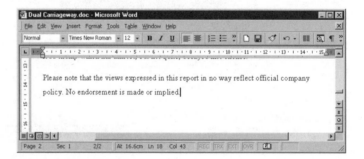

The Spike

You can repeat this more times if necessary. Each time you press Control+F3, any selected text is put onto the Spike.

The Spike is a temporary piece of AutoText which can be added to with a single key command.

Creating a Spike

1 Select some text and type Control+F3 (the text disappears: it has been impaled on the Spike).

2 Repeat the process with a second piece of text.

3 Finally, place the insertion point at the destination for the text and press Control+Shift+F3.

The text is pulled off the Spike and placed back into the document.

AutoComplete

AutoComplete is somewhat akin to AutoText, in that it offers suggestions for the completion of words or phrases that you only need to begin typing. However, while AutoText uses a list of commonly used phrases which have first to be recorded, AutoComplete offers to fill in other sorts of text which can be worked out from the context. For example, AutoComplete can enter:

- the current date

- your or your company's name

- any day of the week

- any month

Begin to type in one of the words or phrases listed above (here we're entering today's date).

If AutoComplete doesn't appear to be functioning, choose "AutoCorrect" from the Tools menu, select the AutoText tab, and make sure there is a tick in the checkbox labelled "Show AutoComplete tip for AutoText and dates".

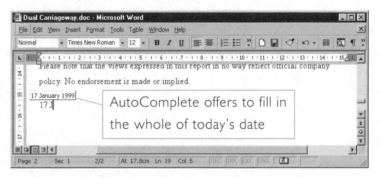

AutoComplete offers to fill in the whole of today's date

To fill in the whole date, simply press Enter or F3.

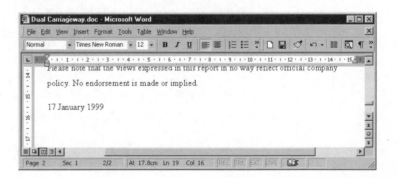

AutoSummarize

This feature uses complex procedures to analyse a document and determine which sentences are likely to carry the document's most significant, salient points. It does this by calculating which words and phrases in the document are used most often. The resulting analysis can then be presented in several different ways.

To use AutoSummarize, do the following:

| Open the document you want to summarize, then choose "AutoSummarize" from the Tools menu. The following dialog box appears:

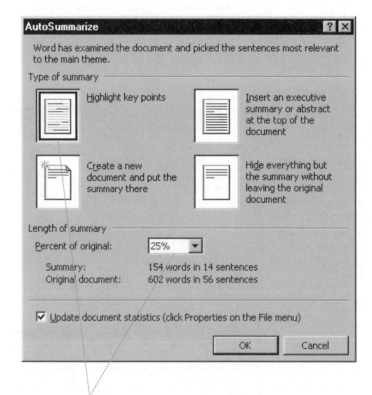

2 Select the way you want to present the summary, and the summary's level of detail, then click "OK".

If the "Highlight key points" option is selected, the whole document is displayed, with the most significant points highlighted. Perform any of the following steps, as appropriate:

3 Click here to toggle between displaying the whole text with the summary highlighted, or the summary only.

4 Click here to increase or decrease the summary's level of detail – i.e. the percentage of the document that is highlighted.

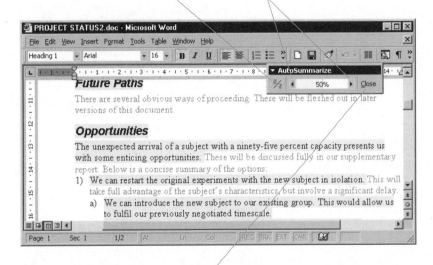

5 Click "Close" to shut down the AutoSummarize control palette and return to the normal document view.

In this example, Word appears to have determined that the headings and initial items in lists have a greater importance.

Hyphenation

You can change the hyphenation options for your document by choosing Tools>Language>Hyphenation:

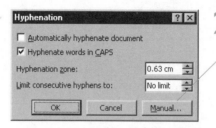

2 If you click on the "Manual" button you can review hyphenation manually throughout your document...

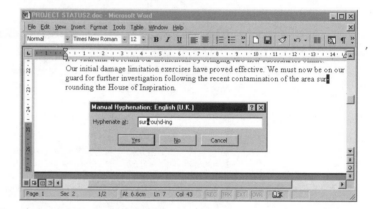

To take even greater control of hyphenation in your text, you may want to use the following keyboard shortcuts:

- *Control+Hyphen will insert an optional hyphen in a word as you type.*
- *Control+Shift+Hyphen will insert a non-breaking hyphen into your text (this is a hyphen where Word is not allowed to break the word over successive lines).*

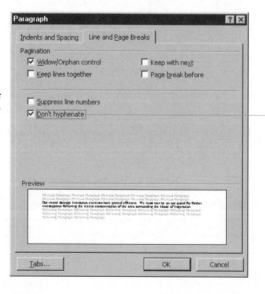

You can also override hyphen-ation for individual paragraphs by selecting the "Don't hyphenate" checkbox in the Line and Page Breaks tab of the Paragraph dialog box (choose "Paragraph" from the "Format" menu).

Templates and Wizards

Templates act as blueprints for standard types of document which you would need to use again and again. Examples may be standard memos, reports, letters or faxes. A Wizard is a "live" document which guides you through its own design.

This chapter shows you how to use templates and Wizards, customise a template for your own purposes, or create a new template.

Covers

Chapter Eight

Using Templates

A template contains a range of settings to be used as a starting point for a new document.

If you select the "New" icon instead of the File menu, Word uses the "Blank Document" or "Normal" template.

The Normal Template

1 Choose "New" from the File menu:

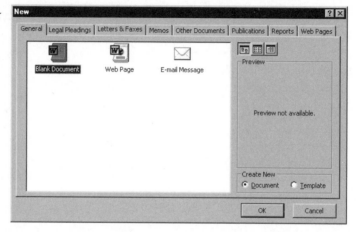

Word lists the templates available. Often you'll use the simple "Blank Document" template.

2 Click on the other tabs to see more available templates.

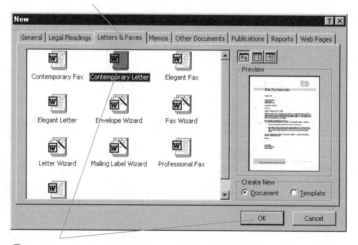

3 Select the template you want to use and click "OK".

Template Defaults

Defaults are settings which are used initially when you create a new document or add new text. To change the defaults for a template, do the following with a template open:

1 Open the Font dialog box from the Format menu.

2 Choose your required settings and then click on the "Default" button.

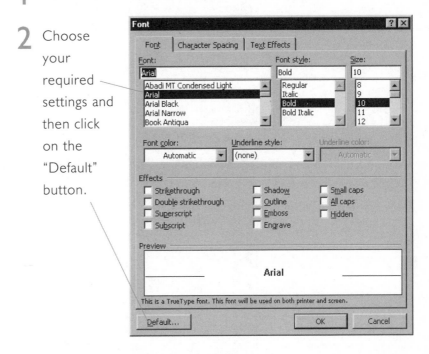

The Office Assistant will ask you whether you're certain that you want to change the Template itself.

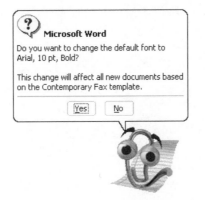

3 If you click "Yes", the font information will be saved into the currently used template document.

Form Templates

By designing a Form Template, you can create a document which is very easy to use, even for people who have minimal experience of Word 2000.

You simply create a document in the normal way, apart from adding some special "form fields". These can be text containers, checkboxes or drop-down selection fields.

Creating Text Form Fields

1 Make sure the Forms palette is active (if necessary, go to the View menu and choose Toolbars).

2 Place your insertion point where you'd like the field, then click on the Text Form Field button in the Forms palette.

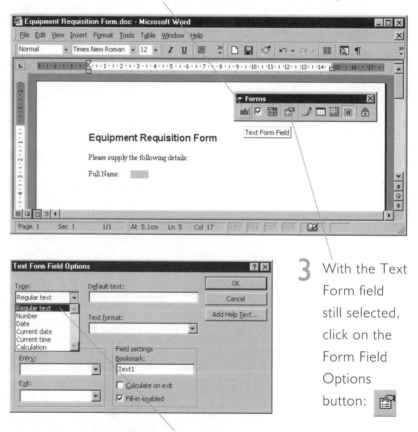

3 With the Text Form field still selected, click on the Form Field Options button:

From here you can select options such as the content type.

Creating Drop-Down Form Fields

Drop-down lists allow users to select from a pop-up restricted list of options. This way they can fill out values within a form without typing anything.

1 Decide where you want the field and position your insertion point accordingly.

2 Click on the Drop-Down Form Field icon in the Forms palette.

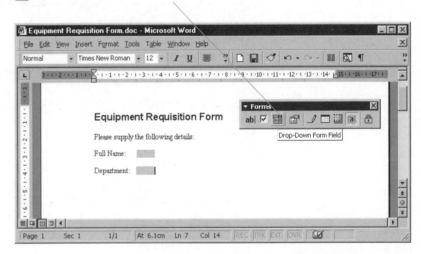

3 With the field still selected, click on the Form Field Options button:

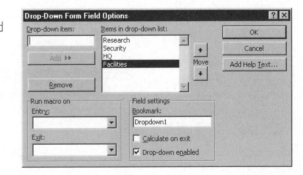

From here you can build the list of options for the drop-down list. Simply enter an item and click the Add button. You can also use the move buttons to reorder the items in the list, or Remove items altogether. When the list is complete, click "OK".

Check Box Form Fields

These act as simple on/off switches for your user. A single-click will toggle a checkmark on and off within the box.

1 Decide where you want the field and position your insertion point accordingly.

2 Click the Check Box Form Field icon in the Forms palette.

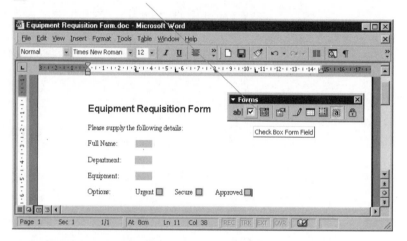

Protecting the Form

Click on the Protect Form icon 🔒 to stop users from editing your document. From now onwards the only items which can be edited are the Form Fields themselves.

Close down the Forms Toolbar when you've completed your form. This will discourage users from attempting to edit the document itself.

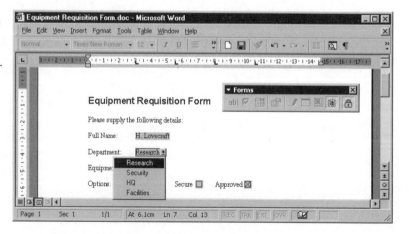

Setting Up a New Template

Any document can be saved as a template, but in this example we'll use the form we've created. With the document open, do the following:

You can also switch protection on and off using the Forms Toolbar. However, from the dialog box, you can additionally set a password. This would prevent others from unprotecting your document.

1 Select "Protect Document" from the Tools menu.

2 Set the Protect option to "Forms".

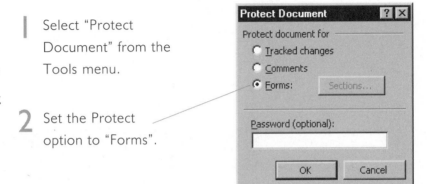

Note that you only need to do this if the template is to be used as a form.

3 Choose "Save As" from the File menu:

If you're using a normal document, rather than a form, you need only follow steps 3 and 4.

4 Choose "Document Template" as the file type.

5 Enter a suitable name for the file and click on Save

The document will automatically be saved with a .DOT extension within Word's Templates folder.

Changing Styles in a Template

When you open a document, Word uses the styles built into the template selected.

As we saw earlier, you can alter these styles for individual documents using the "Style" dialog:

1 Select "Style" from the Format menu.

2 Click on the Modify button to display the following dialog:

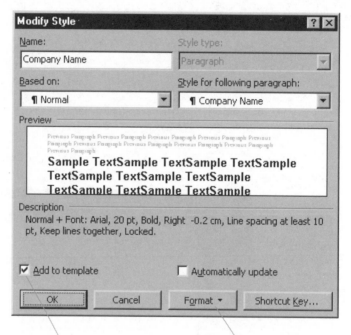

If you record a style change to the "Blank Document" or "Normal" template, this will affect most new documents.

3 To copy a style change back into the template itself, make sure the "Add to Template" box is checked.

4 Make any appropriate changes using the dialogs that can be selected from the Format button pop-up menu.

5 Click "OK".

The Templates and Add-Ins Dialog

Word always keeps track of the template used to create a document. It is possible to change this even after you've started work:

1 If necessary, unprotect your document (Tools menu).

2 Choose "Templates and Add-Ins" from the Tools menu.

You can use the "Add" button to make available styles stored in other templates.

Any templates listed in the "Global" box are always available.

3 Use the "Attach" button to attach a new template. If you select "Automatically update document styles" then the Styles from the new template will be reapplied to the document text.

4 Click "OK" when you're done.

Wizards

A Wizard is a kind of "intelligent" template: it helps you design and build a document by asking you a series of questions. You answer these either by selecting from a choice of radio buttons, or by entering text in a box.

An Example

1 Choose "New" from the File menu, then select this tab.

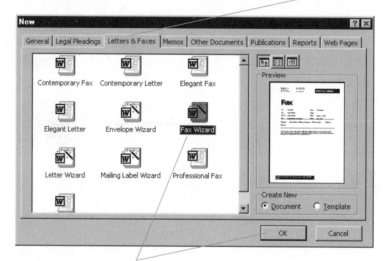

2 Select the "Fax Wizard" icon, then click "OK".

3 Start working through the Wizard by clicking the Next button.

The Fax Wizard is actually capable of sending out faxes directly, provided you have a fax capable modem properly installed in your system. In this example, however, we're instructing the Wizard to create a document which we would firstly print, then send manually using a Fax machine.

4 Each page of the Wizard will ask you more questions. As you work through the pages, the flowchart on the left side will indicate your progress.

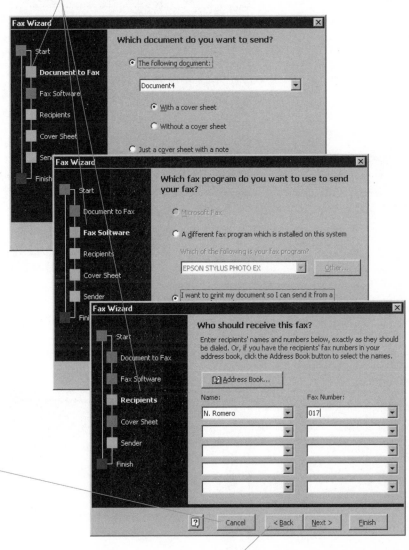

If you decide that this isn't the Wizard for you after all, then click on the Cancel button.

5 At any point you can go back to a previous page simply by clicking the Back button. This way you can fill out the settings in any order you choose.

6 When you have finished making the settings, click on the Finish button.

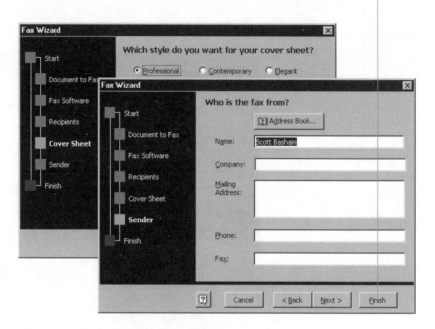

The document is now automatically generated using the settings we supplied. We can continue to edit this manually, if appropriate, then save or print in the normal way.

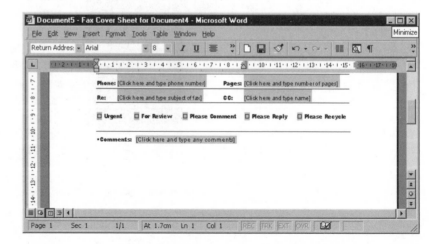

Graphical Features

Although not a full-blown graphics package, Word contains a comprehensive collection of clip art and a respectable range of graphical editing features. This chapter takes you through the processes involved in incorporating pictures and illustrations into your document.

Covers

Chapter Nine

Inserting Pictures from Disk

Word 2000 has its own folder of clip art illustrations, but you can also import from a wide range of graphic file formats.

1 Click the insertion point at the destination for the graphic.

2 Go to the Insert menu, choose "Picture" and "From File".

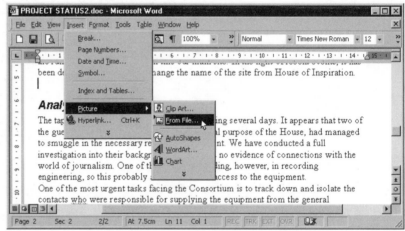

3 Locate the file you require and click "Insert".

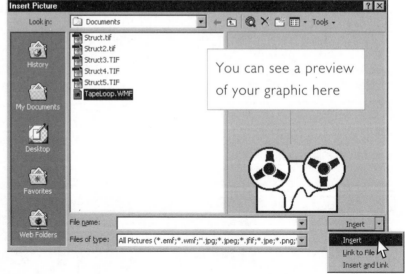

You can see a preview of your graphic here

The picture is inserted into the document:

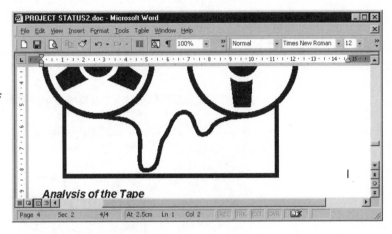

Don't worry if the picture appears in the wrong size. It is easy to resize, as you will see on the next page.

Types of Graphic File

Word can import many types of graphic file format. WMF, CGM, WPG, DRW, EPS and PCT files normally contain Draw-type objects which can be scaled up or down with no loss in quality, because they are stored as vectors (mathematical objects).

On the other hand BMP, PCX, TIF, JPG and GIF files are bitmapped: the image is stored as a structure of tiny dots or blocks. Be careful not to enlarge these pictures too much, or the dots will become very noticeable, causing a marked deterioration in quality.

If you have a scanner or a digital camera installed in your system then you can scan directly into Word. Choose "Insert" then "Picture" and "From Scanner or Camera".

Manipulating Graphics

When you click on a graphic you will see eight blocks appear around it: one at each corner, and one at the middle of each side. These are the graphic's control handles, which can be used to change its dimensions.

I Click on the graphic to make its handles appear.

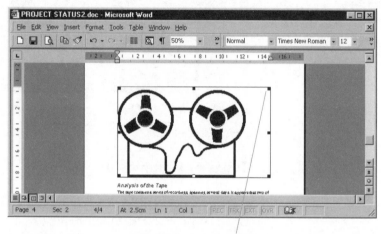

2 Drag on a handle to resize the picture.

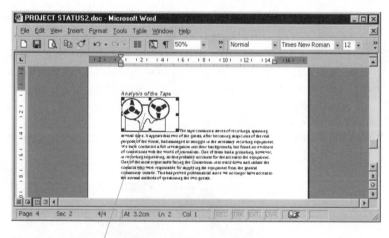

3 To move, drag anywhere within the object.

Note that the graphic is treated like a text item, so when you drag it to a new position, the surrounding text moves to make room.

The Picture Toolbar

The Picture toolbar appears when you insert a picture into a document and provides an easy way to make a wide range of changes to your pictures. It can be used for these functions:

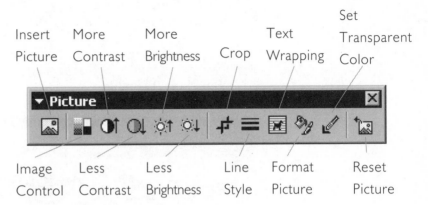

Insert Picture

More Contrast

More Brightness

Crop

Text Wrapping

Set Transparent Color

Image Control

Less Contrast

Less Brightness

Line Style

Format Picture

Reset Picture

Cropping a Picture

If you want to display only part of an image in your Word document, you should crop it. This cuts away a part of the picture from any of its four sides.

1 Select the image.

2 Click on the Crop icon in the Picture toolbar.

Cropping is non-destructive (i.e. you can restore the rest of the picture by dragging the edges back with the Crop tool, or by clicking on the Reset Picture icon).

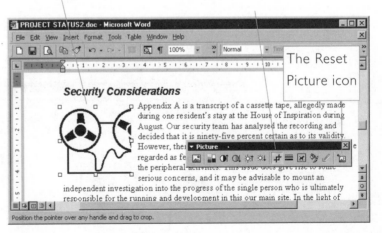

3 Rest your cursor over any of the picture's control handles, then drag the edges to where you want them.

Editing an Imported Picture

Most normal clip art pictures that you import will be in vector format (they'll usually have the .WMF extension), which means that they can be broken down into simple, individual elements which can be edited separately. To edit a vector clip art image, simply do the following:

1 Right-click on the image in your Word document and choose "Edit Picture".

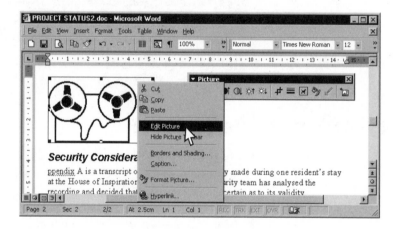

2 You will now find that the clip art object is in fact composed of several different objects, which can be selected individually. Click on one, then try stretching or deleting it.

If you extend the picture beyond its normal bounding rectangle, click this button to reset the picture boundary:

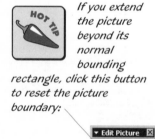

This also applies if you reduce it in size.

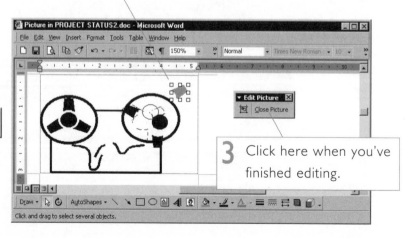

3 Click here when you've finished editing.

Wrapping Text Around Graphics

When a graphic is inserted into a Word document, it is placed into the text by default as a simple object, on a new line. However, you can very easily change this, so that text wraps around the image in any of a number of ways:

1 Select the picture.

2 Click on the Text Wrapping icon in the Picture toolbar, and select how you want the text to wrap around the image.

If the Picture toolbar is not visible, select "Toolbars" from the View menu, and choose "Picture".

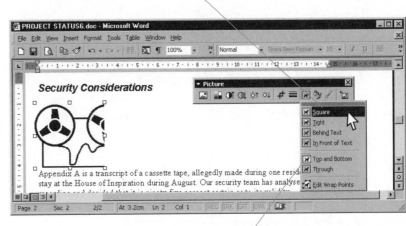

This is the default text wrap

The text now wraps around the image. This is "Square" wrap: the text wraps around a rectangular area that borders the graphic.

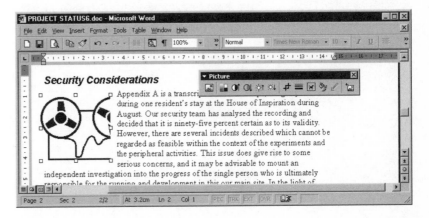

The Format Picture Dialog

From here you can numerically change all the properties of a graphic, including its size, position, text-wrap properties and crop parameters.

| Select the picture.

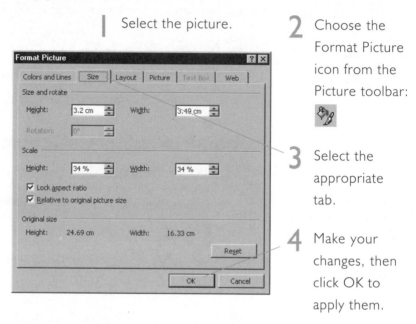

2 Choose the Format Picture icon from the Picture toolbar:

3 Select the appropriate tab.

4 Make your changes, then click OK to apply them.

The Drawing Toolbar

Click here to see other drawing-related commands, as shown below:

When working with graphics in Word 2000, you are not limited to using ready-made clip art; you can create your own drawings using Word's Drawing toolbar.

To display the Drawing toolbar, click on the Drawing icon in the Standard toolbar, or select View>Toolbars>Drawing:

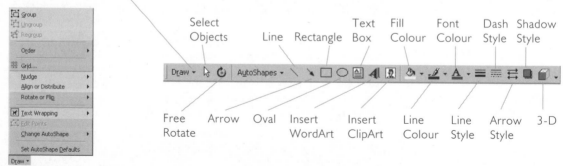

Select Objects Line Rectangle Text Box Fill Colour Font Colour Dash Style Shadow Style

Free Rotate Arrow Oval Insert WordArt Insert ClipArt Line Colour Line Style Arrow Style 3-D

Creating Shapes

1 Select the appropriate shape tool.

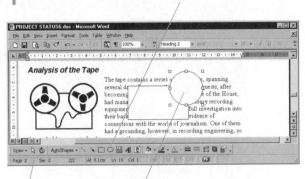

2 Click and drag within the document to create the shape. For lines, drag from one end-point to the other; for boxes and ovals drag diagonally from one corner to the other.

3 Click on a shape with the pointer to select it. Then you can drag it to another location, or resize it by dragging directly on one of its handles.

Lines and Fills

Click on a shape then use the Fill and Line pop-up menus to select colour, shading and line patterns.

Click on the arrow to the right of the icon to produce the pop-up menu

Click here to add special effects to the object's fill

These properties can also be changed via the Format AutoShape dialog box: right-click on a shape, then select Format AutoShape from the pop-up menu.

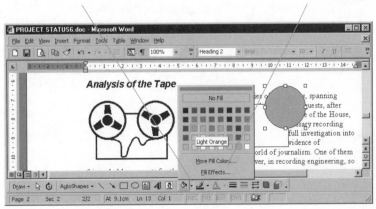

AutoShapes

AutoShapes allow you to insert commonly used shapes, many of which otherwise might take you some time to draw. To insert an AutoShape, do the following:

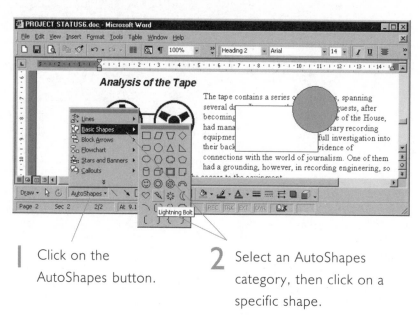

1 Click on the AutoShapes button.

2 Select an AutoShapes category, then click on a specific shape.

3 Click in the area of your document where you want the AutoShape to appear.

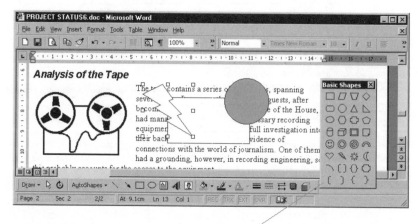

Free-floating Shapes palette

Formatting Shapes

Many objects' properties can be amended by accessing the pop-up menus in the Drawing toolbar. However, by right-clicking on a shape you can summon a dialog box that allows you to change many of these properties straight away. Right-click on the AutoShape whose format you want to change, choose "Format AutoShape" from the pop-up menu, then select the appropriate tab...

To set the properties for more than one shape, you should first select all the shapes you want to change. To do this, you have two options:

- *Click successively on each object while holding down the Shift button, or;*

- *Click in the document area and drag a selection box around all of the objects*

Once all the objects are selected, change the properties as you would for a single object (e.g. right-click on any object, then select "Format AutoShape" from the pop-up menu).

The Colors and Lines Tab
Use this to set the shape's fill and line attributes.

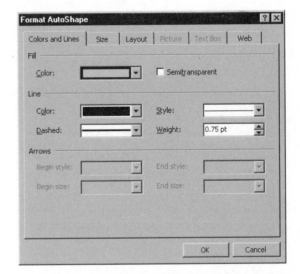

The Size Tab
Use this to set the shape's dimensions, scale properties and rotation value.

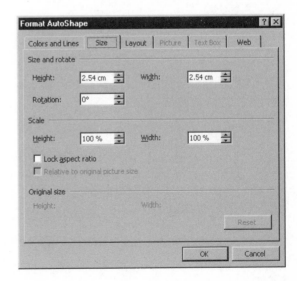

The Layout Tab

From here you can control the way text wraps around the AutoShape.

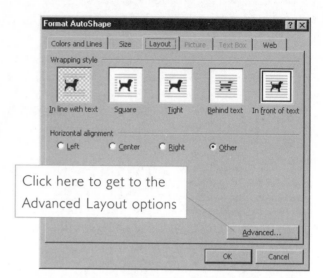

Click here to get to the Advanced Layout options

Advanced Layout

Here you can set the coordinates used to determine the object's precise position on the page.

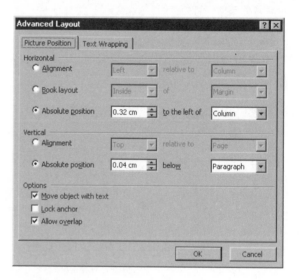

Setting AutoShape Defaults

To set the properties that all AutoShapes will have when they are created, do the following:

1. Format an existing AutoShape using the Drawing toolbar or the Format AutoShape dialog.

2. Right-click on the shape, then select Set AutoShape Defaults.

Changing Object Order

When you place a new image or shape in a document, it appears in front of all the other objects that were inserted before it. To change the relative order of objects subsequently, select the object(s) to move, then...

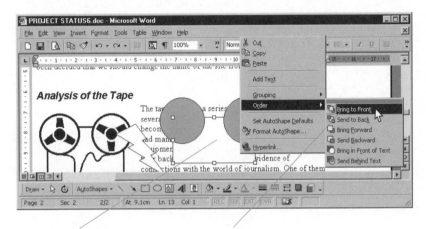

1 Right-click on one of the shapes and choose "Order" from the pop-up menu.

2 Choose whether to send the object in front of or behind all other objects, or whether to move it just one step.

Sending Objects Behind the Text Layer

By default, all graphic objects appear in front of the text in your document. However, you can send objects behind the text by selecting "Bring in Front of Text" or "Send Behind Text" from the "Order" submenu:

Grouping and Ungrouping

Once you have placed several objects in your Word document, you may no longer need to treat them separately, but might benefit from treating them as a single object which can be moved and modified easily. To make this possible, you should group the objects, as follows:

1 Select all of the objects that you want to be grouped together.

2 Choose "Group" from the pop-up Draw menu in the Drawing toolbar.

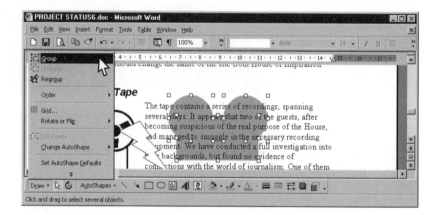

Subsequently, any changes made to the group are applied to all of the grouped objects:

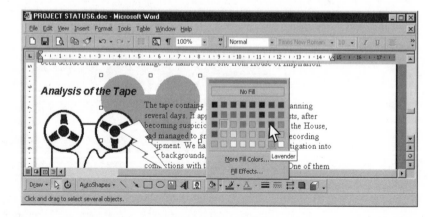

WordArt

WordArt is a tool you can use to apply a wide range of special graphical effects to type that you use in your Word documents. The objects created by WordArt are treated not as plain text but as drawing objects, so they can be manipulated further with the tools from the Drawing toolbar. To use WordArt, do the following:

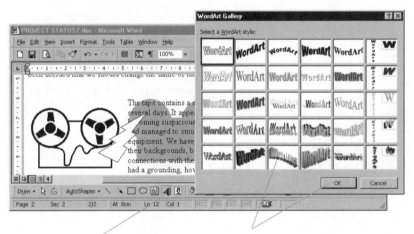

1 Click on the WordArt button in the Drawing toolbar.

2 Select a style (you can change it later), then click "OK".

3 Enter your text here, then click "OK".

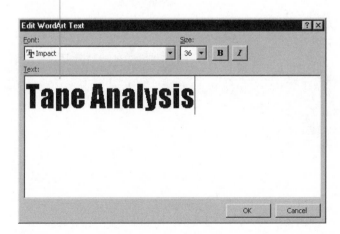

The WordArt is placed, and can now be edited:

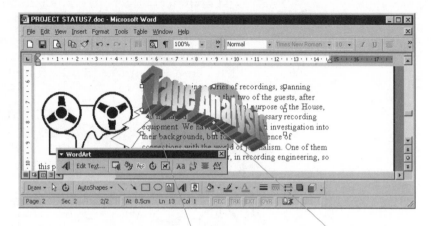

4 Click on the text with the cursor and drag it to the desired position.

5 Drag on the text's control handles to change its size.

6 Drag on these special yellow handles to alter the characteristics of the effect.

When you select the "Change WordArt shape" icon, you are presented with a palette containing 40 different text shapes. This offers a wider range of shapes than the Gallery:

The floating WordArt toolbar appears whenever you select a WordArt object. You can use it for the following functions:

Return to the text-editing box encountered in step 3

Open the Format dialog to alter colour, size, position, text wrap

Allow text to be rotated freely

Edit text wrapping

Toggle between horizontal and vertical text

Add a new WordArt item

Return to the WordArt Gallery dialog (step 2)

Change WordArt shape

Make upper- and lowercase letters same height

Change character spacing

Change text alignment

Tables and Charts

Tables allow you to organise and manage text in rows and columns. Charts provide a valuable way of presenting numeric table information in pictorial form, making statistical information much easier to understand.

Covers

Chapter Ten

Inserting a Table

If you want to insert a simple table with more than five columns or four rows, select "Insert Table" from the Table menu. This will summon a dialog box, where you can specify the table's dimensions.

If you want to insert a simple table of no more than five columns and four rows, you can use the Table icon in the Standard toolbar:

1 Place the insertion point on a blank line in the document.

2 Click on the Table icon in the Standard toolbar and, in the pop-up table box, drag downwards and to the right.

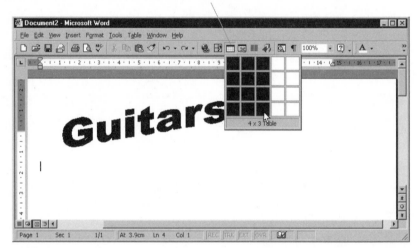

The further you drag, the larger the table. In this case a table of 4 rows and 3 columns is being created.

The table is inserted into your document:

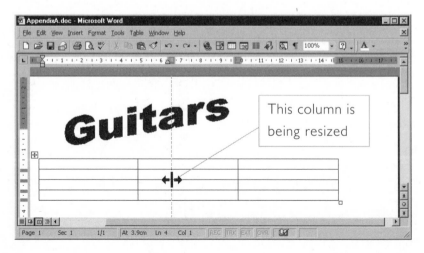

You can resize a column by moving your Mouse pointer to the border between the columns: it will turn into a black double headed arrow ←|→. You can resize rows in the same way.

Hold down the Alt key while dragging a column or row to see the measurements in the ruler.

Drawing a Table

Word 2000 offers you an alternative method to create tables. The Draw Table tool lets you draw a table directly into your document without using dialogs or pop-up boxes.

| Select "Draw Table" from the Table menu. The Tables and Borders toolbar appears:

There is an alternative way to begin drawing a table and specify the width of its columns visually: in normal text-entry mode, enter a line using plus and minus symbols, like this...

+---+------+------+

When you press Return, Word will automatically convert this into the first line of a table, the plus signs becoming column boundaries. If this doesn't work, select Tools> AutoCorrect, choose the "AutoFormat As You Type" tab, and check the "Tables" box.

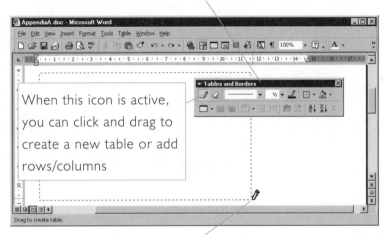

When this icon is active, you can click and drag to create a new table or add rows/columns

2 Your pointer will turn into a pencil shape (if not then make sure that the Draw Table tool is active). Drag an initial shape for the table within your document.

3 Click and drag anywhere in your table to draw a column or row boundary.

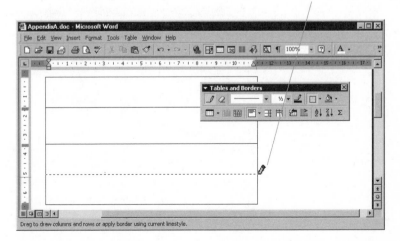

Drawing Diagonal Table Lines

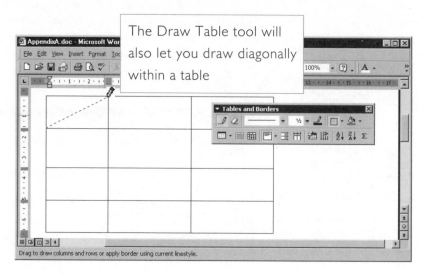

The Draw Table tool will also let you draw diagonally within a table

Erasing Table Lines

Click on the Eraser tool in the Tables and Borders palette.

Your cursor turns into an eraser shape.

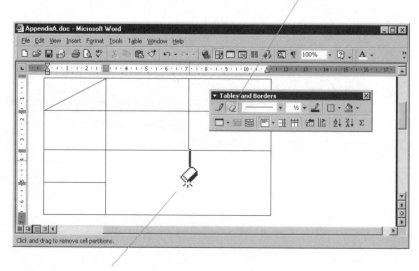

2 Click directly on a line within the table to make it disappear.

Creating Irregular Tables

The table drawing tools make it easy for you to create irregularly structured tables.

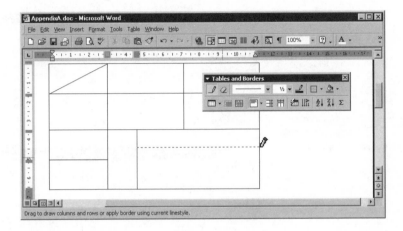

Entering Text

You can add text to your table by clicking in each cell in turn. All the normal formatting commands still apply. A quick way to get to the next cell is to press Tab. Shift+Tab takes you back to the previous cell.

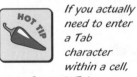

If you actually need to enter a Tab character within a cell, press Control+Tab.

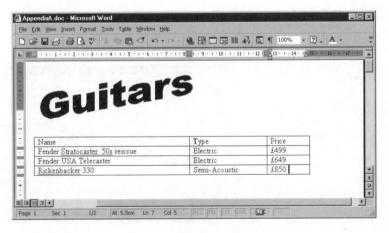

You can have more than one line within each cell. The Table row will expand to accommodate any extra text.

Formatting

You can format the contents of a whole row or column – or several rows or columns – at once. To select a row, drag across it, or click in the space just to its left.

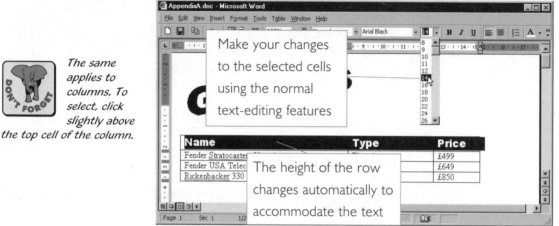

Inserting a Row/Column

To insert a row into an existing table, do the following:

1 Select the line below where you want the new row.

2 Click the right Mouse button on the selected row, and choose "Insert Rows" from the pop-up menu.

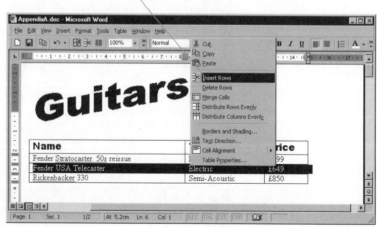

Cutting and Pasting

I Select the row/column or cells.

2 Right-click on the selected cells and choose "Cut" from the pop-up menu.

3 Select the destination row/ column or cells.

4 Right click on the selected cells and choose "Paste..." from the pop-up menu.

The text is pasted back into the table, immediately above the selected row, or to the left of the selected column.

Merging Cells

Any number of adjacent cells can be merged to create a single cell, by selecting the cells and then choosing "Merge Cells" from the Table menu.

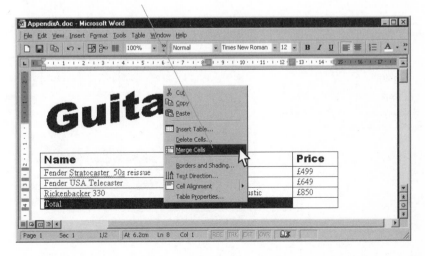

Controlling Height and Width

To select an entire table, choose "Select", then "Table" from the Table menu, or type Alt + Numeric keypad "5" with the Num Lock turned off.

1 Select the cell(s) to change, or the entire table.

2 Choose "Table Properties" from the Table menu, or by right clicking.

3 Click on the Row tab, then the Column tab to see all the options available.

4 The Table Tab will let you set properties such as overall size, alignment and text wrap behaviour.

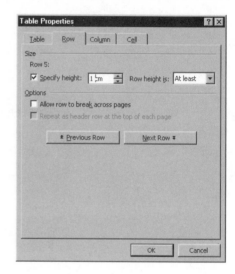

Nested Tables

This feature is new to Word 2000. You can now insert a table within another table. You can draw the inner table in the normal way with the Draw Table tool:

Another way to create a nested table is to right click on the destination cell and choose Insert Table. You can also cut, copy and paste entire tables.

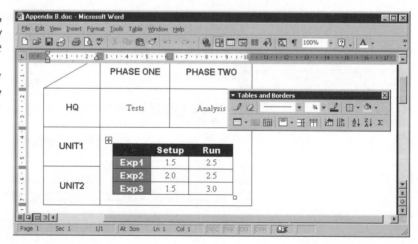

Formulae

If you want one cell of a table to display a number derived from a calculation (based on the numeric contents of other cells), Word can insert a code to perform this task automatically. In this example, we want to total the price of the three guitars in the table.

For the Sum function to work properly, all rows above the current cell must have the same number of columns. If you merged the cells for the last example, you will need to split them again (choose "Split Cells" from the Table menu).

1   Click in the cell which is the destination for the calculation, and choose "Formula" from the Table menu.

2   Enter the formula or select from the list of "Paste functions". Word correctly suggests the "=SUM(ABOVE)" function, which adds up the contents of the cells above the destination cell.

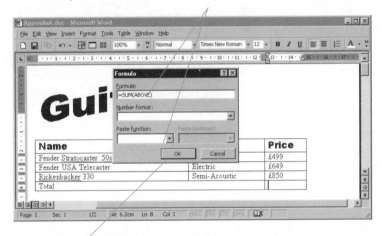

Unlike a spreadsheet (such as Excel), Word does not automatically update the contents of cells containing a formula when the values of cells used in the equation are changed. To update a formula, right-click on the cell and choose "Update Field" from the pop-up menu.

3   Click "OK". The total is displayed in the destination cell:

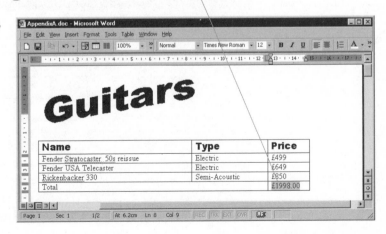

Borders and Shading

Word 2000 allows you to enhance your tables very easily using the Borders and Shading dialog. To use it, do the following:

1 Select either the entire table or just a range of cells.

2 Right-click on the selected cells and choose "Borders and Shading" from the pop-up menu.

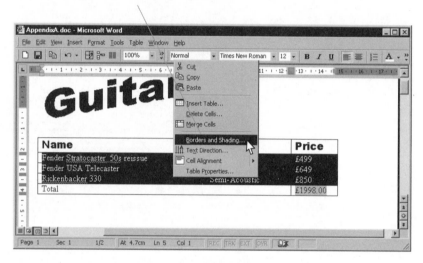

3 If necessary, activate the Borders tab and choose your borders options.

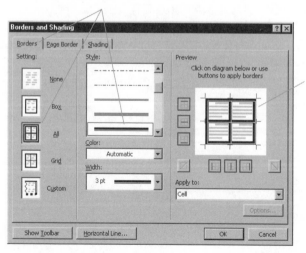

You can click on various parts of this diagram to activate different perimeter and internal lines

4 Now click on the Shading tab and set your shading
preferences.

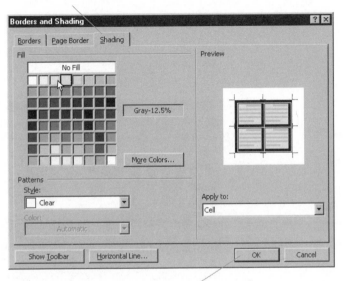

5 Click "OK". Your selected cells now have a border and
shading applied:

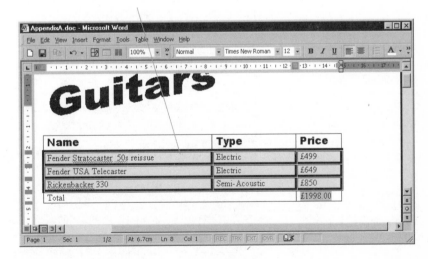

In the example above, the Borders and Shading dialog box
has been used to alter the style of all the lines in the selected
area, and to give those cells a fill of 12.5% grey.

Table AutoFormat

As an alternative to defining the format piece by piece (i.e., specifying the font, borders, shading, etc.), Word 2000 allows you to apply many different pre-defined formats to existing tables. To use AutoFormat, do the following:

1 Select the table.

2 Choose "Table AutoFormat" from the Table menu, or click on this button.

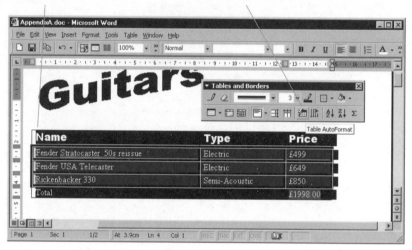

The following dialog appears:

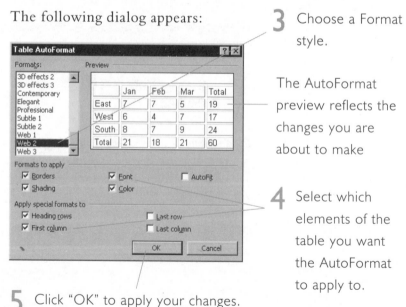

3 Choose a Format style.

The AutoFormat preview reflects the changes you are about to make

4 Select which elements of the table you want the AutoFormat to apply to.

5 Click "OK" to apply your changes.

The changes that you have just specified are applied automatically to your table:

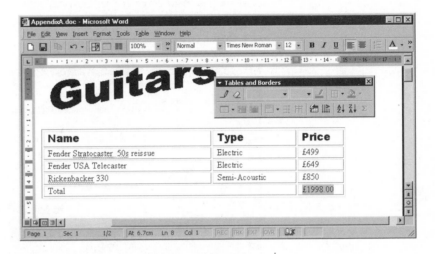

Using the Tables and Borders Toolbar

You can use the Tables and Borders toolbar to make many of the formatting changes that we have discussed earlier in this chapter. If it is not already activated, select View>Toolbars>Tables and Borders, or click on the appropriate icon in the Standard toolbar:

The Tables and Borders toolbar offers the following functions:

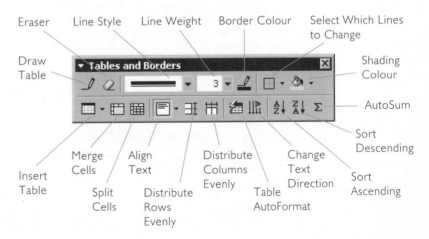

Graphics within Tables

With Word 2000 you can paste or insert graphics directly into cells. Once there you can right-click on the graphic and choose Format Picture to control properties such as text wrap. In the example below, text and graphics coexist within the same cell.

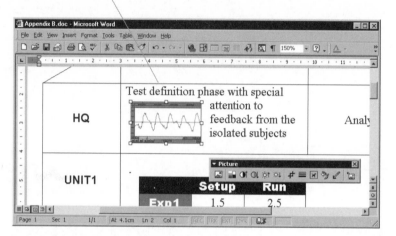

Text Wrap around Tables

If you right-click on a table and choose Table Properties, you can control how text wraps around the table itself. In the example below, a text wrap setting of "Around" allows the table to be included within the main text area.

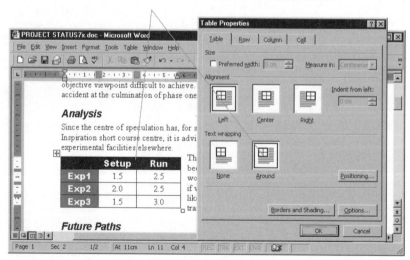

Creating a Chart from a Table

You can use the Microsoft Graph 2000 feature to convert a table you have created into an attractive chart.

1 Select the data in the table.

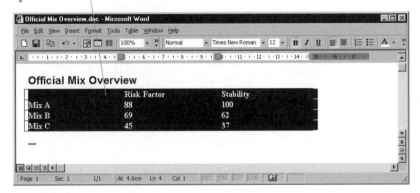

2 Choose "Object" from the Insert Menu.

3 Choose "Microsoft Graph 2000 Chart" from the Create New tab of the Object dialog, then click "OK".

You can also activate the Chart application by clicking on the Chart tool button:

If this is not visible, then right-click on a toolbar and choose "Customise". The Chart icon is available under the "Insert" category. From here you can drag it onto any toolbar.

Microsoft Graph 2000 automatically generates a suitable graph based on your data, and places it in your document:

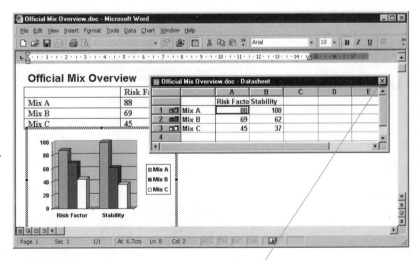

4 If you don't want to amend your data yet, close this window.

Formatting a Chart

Once your chart is placed in your document, you can very easily edit it to amend the format that Microsoft Graph applied by default.

1 Double-click on the chart to open it for editing. A striped border appears around it, and special Microsoft Graph icons appear in the toolbar.

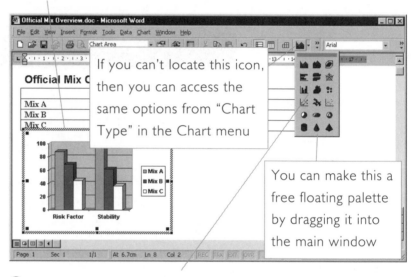

If you can't locate this icon, then you can access the same options from "Chart Type" in the Chart menu

You can make this a free floating palette by dragging it into the main window

Microsoft Graph 2000 uses two main windows, one for the data and one for the chart itself. You can turn the Datasheet on and off using the View menu, or the Datasheet icon on the toolbar:

2 To change the type of chart, click on the arrow to the right of the Chart type icon and select an option from the palette.

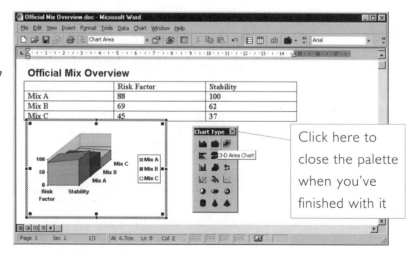

Click here to close the palette when you've finished with it

You can change the number format of any of the data used in your chart. Simply select the relevant cells then choose "Number" from the Format menu. In the "Format number" dialog, select the number type from the "Category:" options, then make any amendments in the context-specific boxes and click OK.

3 To change the properties of a 3D graph, rest your cursor over the chart area until the "Chart Area" bubble appears, then right-click.

4 In the pop-up menu that appears, select "3-D View".

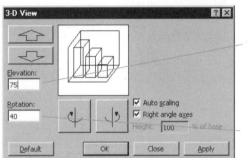

Clicking here would produce a dialog that offers an alternative way of selecting the chart type from the method in step 2

5 Click here to change the elevation of the view.

6 Click here to change the degree of rotation.

When changing the format of a chart, always use the bubbles that appear when you rest your cursor over a chart area. You can then be sure that you are about to format the area that you mean to, before you double-click or right-click on it.

7 To change the properties of an individual chart element, double-click on it. Here, the font properties of the axis legends are being changed.

8 Click "OK" to apply your changes.

Importing Data into a Chart

To import data from an external source into a chart, make sure that it is open for editing (it will have a striped border around it, and the Microsoft Graph toolbar will appear), then do the following:

If there is no striped border around the chart, then double-click directly on it. This will open the chart for editing.

1 Select "Import File" from the Edit menu.

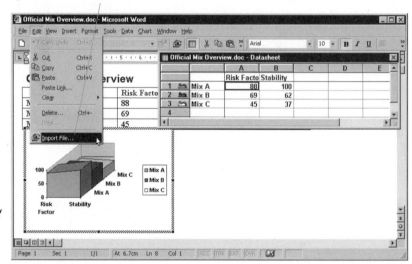

When you are working on a chart, you are effectively using the Microsoft Graph application. This means that the menu options and toolbar icons that you see are relevant only to Microsoft Graph.

To exit this mode and return to the normal Word 2000 environment, simply click your cursor anywhere outside the chart area; the Word toolbars and menu options will then return.

2 In the Import File dialog, select the file you want to import, then click Open.

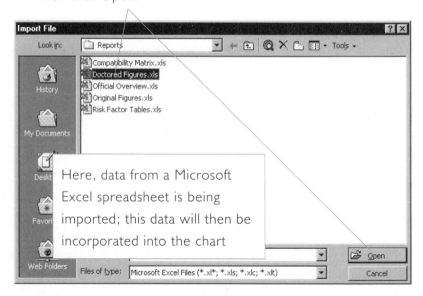

Here, data from a Microsoft Excel spreadsheet is being imported; this data will then be incorporated into the chart

On-line and Internet Documents

Word 2000 contains many new features relating to the Internet and documents intended for viewing on-line. Items normally incorporated into Web pages, such as hyperlinks, can be incorporated into standard Word documents allowing instant access to files stored locally or anywhere on the Internet. Also, HTML is now a native file format to Word 2000, allowing editing of HTML Web pages using Word. The Web Page Wizard will even automatically set up a structure and basic functionality for your pages.

Covers

Chapter Eleven

Introduction

In the past, word-processors were used as tools for producing pure text documents and little else. Recent years have seen popular word-processors become embellished with new graphically-oriented features, which previously would have been found only in high-end Desktop Publishing packages.

Until recently, the aim of most people using a word-processor was to produce something that would ultimately be output on paper. However, the growing importance of the Internet and Intranet environments has seen a change in this situation. Communication which was once conducted on paper is increasingly being carried out in a purely electronic medium.

This electronic communication is carried out in a variety of forms. The World-Wide Web is a vast resource containing endless linked pages, with text and pictures on virtually any topic imaginable. Until recently e-mail had been restricted to text, and remained essentially a means of communicating with a more restricted set of people.

However, these boundaries are beginning to be blurred. Word, for example, allows you to create an electronic document which is not simply text but which may contain animations, pictures, sounds, videos, and links to other documents or Web pages. In fact, any document which you create in Word 2000 (or in any element of Office 2000) may be placed on the Internet. You can even use Word as your primary means of composing and editing e-mail messages.

Word also allows you to create Web pages in the Web's native format, HTML (HyperText Mark-up Language), without having to learn the many HTML codes. You can either use the Web Page Wizard to create a new set of HTML documents quickly and easily, or you can convert an existing Word document.

Using the Web Page Wizard

The Web Page Wizard is the most effective way of using Word to create an HTML document, and allows you more control over the finished product than you would have if you converted an existing Word document. To launch it, do the following:

1 Select New from the File menu.

2 Select the Web Pages tab.

3 Double-click here.

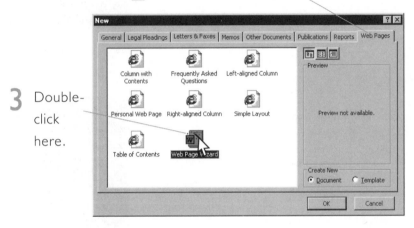

The Web Page Wizard dialog appears. This will guide you through five steps, asking questions about your planned document.

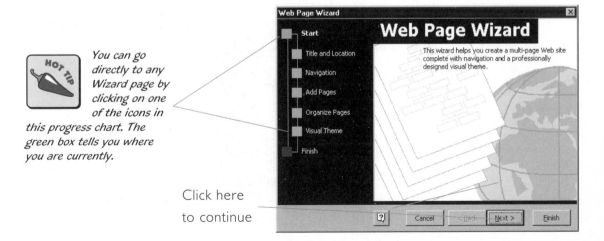

You can go directly to any Wizard page by clicking on one of the icons in this progress chart. The green box tells you where you are currently.

Click here to continue

...cont'd

4 Enter a title
for your
Web site.

*By default this
title will be
used as the
directory for
your Web files,
within "my documents".
However, you can change it
by editing this field.*

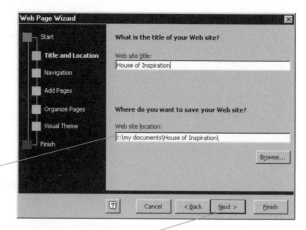

Click "Next" when you're ready

*The "frame"
options split
the screen into
two sections:
one for
navigation and one for
content.*

5 Next, choose
a navigation
model, then
click "Next".

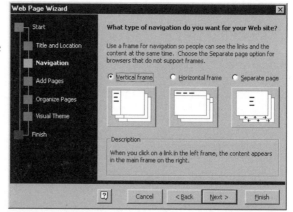

*As long as the
Wizard is still
running, you
can always
return here to
add or remove pages from
the list.*

6 By default,
the Wizard
will create
three pages.
Click here to
add more.

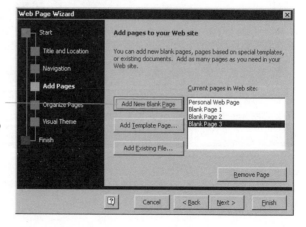

7 From here you can rename your pages, and change their order.

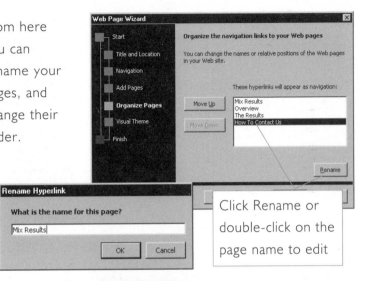

Click Rename or double-click on the page name to edit

8 Finally, you can select a Theme to give your Web pages a consistent look and feel.

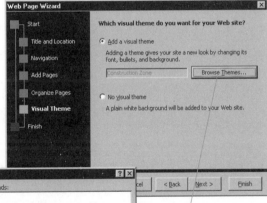

See Chapter 5, *"Styles and Themes"*, for more information about Themes.

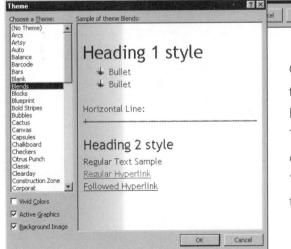

Click here to see the Themes dialog box. Choose a Theme and its options, then click "OK" to return to the Wizard.

9 You are now ready to generate your Web site. Click the Finish button.

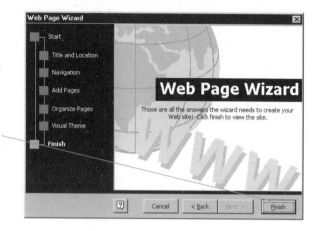

The Wizard now generates the necessary Web pages, saved as .HTM files in the directory specified in step 4. You can view these directly in your Web browser by choosing its Open file option. However, Word's Web layout view will let you view and edit .HTM files.

The Web pages are automatically connected using hyperlinks created by the Wizard. For example, clicking on the Overview hyperlink will cause the main content frame to load up the Overview.htm file.

Now that the Wizard has set up the initial Web document, it is up to you to edit the actual text to your own needs. Word has put placeholder information in each significant area of each page. You simply change and add to this sample text.

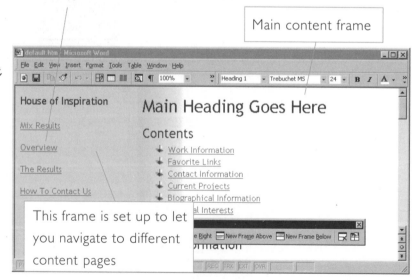

Frames

Frames allow you to divide your screen into rectangular areas, each of which can be used to view a different Web page (or a different part of the same Web page). In our example the Wizard has set up two frames: the left frame is used for navigation while the right shows the main content.

The Frames Toolbar

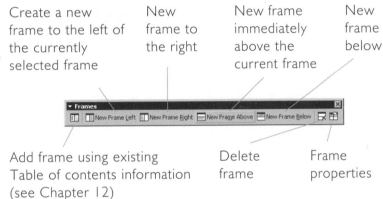

Create a new frame to the left of the currently selected frame

New frame to the right

New frame immediately above the current frame

New frame below

Add frame using existing Table of contents information (see Chapter 12)

Delete frame

Frame properties

Adding a New Frame

Here we've clicked on the New Frame Above button to add a new frame along the top of the document. We'll use this to display a constant header for our pages.

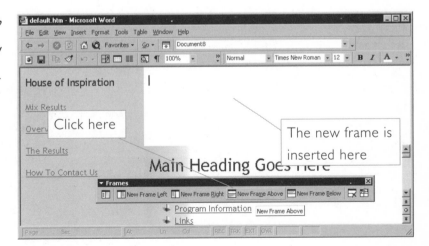

Adding Text and Graphics to a Frame

Once you've added a frame, it behaves like an independent document, so you can add and edit text or other objects in the normal way.

In the example below we've inserted a picture from a file and also incorporated some WordArt.

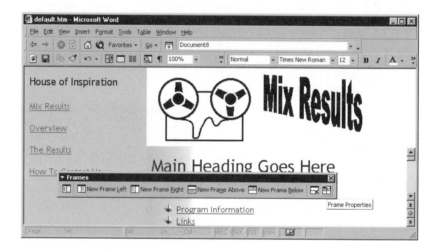

The Frame Properties Dialog

1 Make sure your insertion point is somewhere inside the relevant Frame.

2 Click on the Frame Properties button in the Frames toolbar.

3 From the Frames Tab you can set the name, size and Web page. From the Borders tab you can switch on the Frames border, allowing users to resize the Frame.

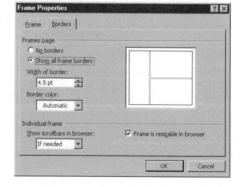

You can also access this dialog box by right-clicking inside a Frame and choosing "Frame Properties".

4 Click OK. In this example the user can now resize the frame by dragging directly on the border.

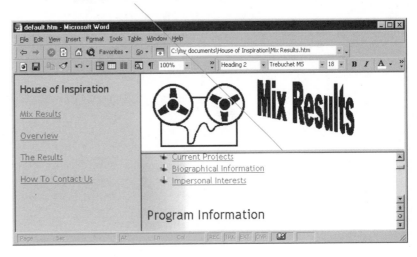

Alternative Text

It is important to remember that some Web Browsers do not display graphics. Furthermore, because graphics take much longer to download from the Web, a user may decide to switch off a graphic display preference. In these cases, you can set text to be displayed as an alternative.

Alternative text also displays while a picture is loading. You may want to include the graphic's file size to give your users an idea of how long the loading process will take.

1 Right-click on the graphic and choose "Format Picture" from the pop-up menu.

2 Click on the Web tab and enter the text.

The Web Tools Palette

Word 2000 provides you with a powerful set of tools to enhance your Web pages. This can be activated just like any other palette, either using the View menu or by right-clicking on an existing Toolbar.

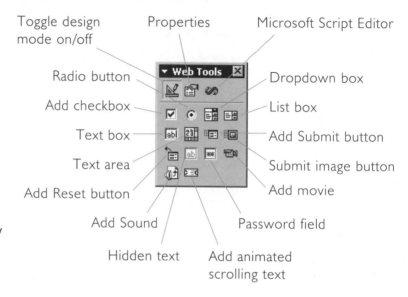

Toggle design mode on/off — Properties — Microsoft Script Editor

Radio button — Dropdown box

Add checkbox — List box

Text box — Add Submit button

Text area — Submit image button

Add Reset button — Add movie

Add Sound — Password field

Hidden text — Add animated scrolling text

As soon as you select one of the tools for adding objects to your Web page, Word 2000 automatically activates design mode.

Design Mode

When design mode is active you can add, edit or delete objects such as radio buttons or text boxes.

When design mode is inactive you can test out your objects. Clicking on a check box, for example, will switch its checkmark on and off.

For more details about how to write and edit Scripts, refer to the Microsoft Development Environment online Help.

Microsoft Script Editor

This allows you to add functionality to your Web page by adding scripts written in Microsoft Visual Basic® (scripting edition) or JScript® (Java Script).

Adding Video Clips

Most Web pages are a collection of text, images and links to other pages. However, as the multimedia capabilities of PCs increase, other types of media are becoming ever more common on the Web. For example, you can place video clips on your Web pages.

1 Place the cursor where you want to insert your video.

2 Click on the Add Movie button 📷 in the Web toolbar.

You can add a movie to a normal document by choosing Object from the Insert menu.

3 Select the file name of the video you want to insert.

4 You can set an alternate image to be displayed if the browser doesn't support video playback, or if it is disabled by the user.

5 Set the Start and Loop options, then click OK.

The video clip appears at your insertion point.

6 You can alter the size of the video in the normal way by dragging on its control handles.

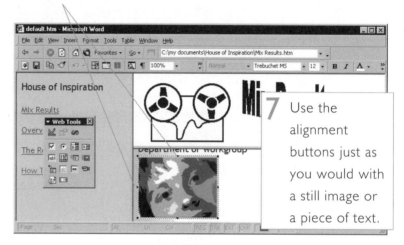

7 Use the alignment buttons just as you would with a still image or a piece of text.

Adding Sound

You can add background music or sound recordings to your web page just as easily as adding the video. Word 2000 allows you to use files in a number of formats including WAV and MIDI files. Whenever someone accesses your page, this file is played providing the browser allows background music, and also if a suitable driver for the type of sound file has been installed.

1 Click on the Sound icon in the Web toolbar.

2 Select the required sound file then click "Open".

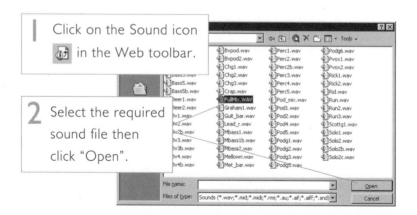

3 Set the looping option then click "OK".

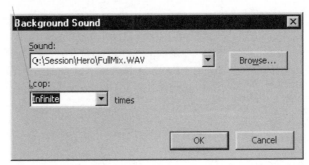

In this example the file FullMix.WAV will play and repeat indefinitely as long as the user is working with the current Web page.

Measuring Using Pixels

When working with Web pages, the computer screen is the primary output device. It is therefore much more convenient to measure objects in pixels rather than units like centimetres or inches.

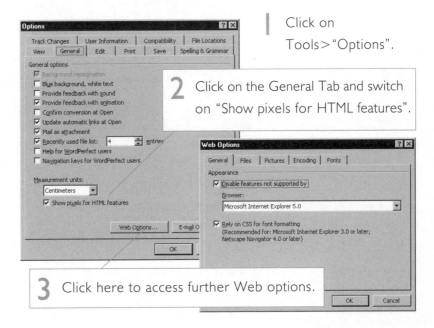

1 Click on Tools > "Options".

2 Click on the General Tab and switch on "Show pixels for HTML features".

3 Click here to access further Web options.

Hyperlinks

If Word doesn't convert link addresses like this to hyperlinks by underlining them and changing their colour, you may need to change your AutoFormat settings. Choose AutoCorrect from the Tools menu, then select the "AutoFormat As You Type" tab. Make sure the "Replace... Internet and network paths with hyperlinks" option is checked.

In the earlier topic "Using the Web Page Wizard" (page 151), hyperlinks were used to provide a method of moving between one HTML document and another. In Word 2000 you are not restricted to using hyperlinks in HTML pages. You can place them in any normal Word document to link to another place in the same document, to another Word document on your hard drive/local network, or even to a file anywhere on the Internet/Intranet.

AutoFormatting Hyperlinks As You Type

By default, Word 2000's AutoFormat feature will automatically convert any piece of text that looks like an Internet address or other file location to a hyperlink. These addresses must be in the standard URL format, with which you will be familiar if you have any experience of using a Web browser:

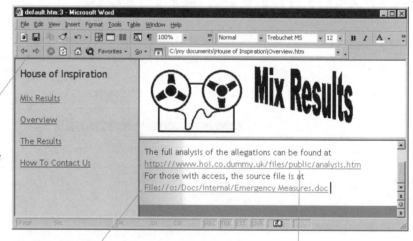

Click on these arrows to move backwards and forwards through documents and Web pages you have visited recently.

This is a link to a Word file on the same hard drive as the current document. Note the prefix "File://" is needed for Word to recognise this as a file location.

This is an Internet URL, linking to a Web site. You must be connected to the Internet for this link to work.

Inserting Hyperlinks Manually

The AutoFormat method is fine for converting actual
Internet addresses and file locations to hyperlinks, but most
hyperlink markers do not take this format; instead the
hyperlink is represented by some more meaningful text, or
even an image. You can use Word to make either of these
into a hyperlink.

1 Select the text or image that the user will click on to jump to
your linked file or Web site.

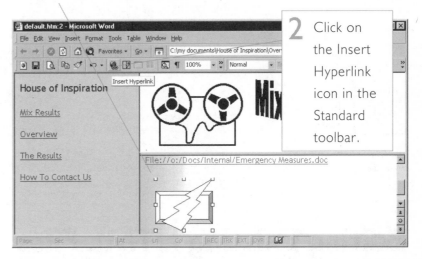

2 Click on
the Insert
Hyperlink
icon in the
Standard
toolbar.

3 Type or select the name of the file you wish to link to. This
can be a file or a Web page. Use the Browse buttons to
search in a
particular
location.

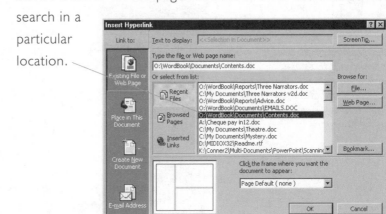

Saving HTML Files

HTML is a native file format for Word 2000. This means that you can open, edit and save in .HTM format just as easily as the .DOC files more traditionally associated with Word.

If you have just created some Web pages from scratch, you will need to choose "Save as Web Page" from the File menu.

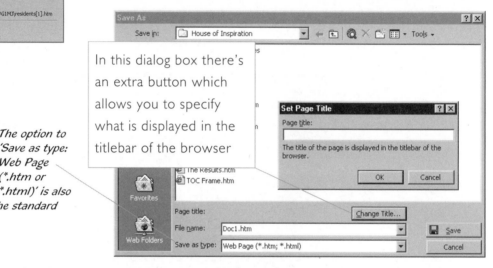

In this dialog box there's an extra button which allows you to specify what is displayed in the titlebar of the browser

The option to 'Save as type: Web Page (*.htm or *.html)' is also available in the standard Save dialog.

Editing Existing HTML Files

Some specialist programs, such as Microsoft FrontPage, allow you to design Web pages using advanced effects like animated buttons. You can still take the files produced by FrontPage and edit them using Word.

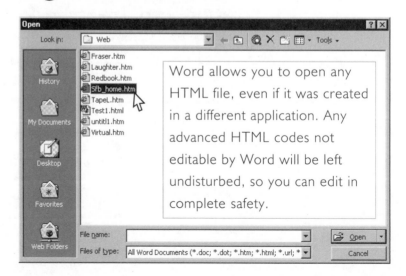

Word allows you to open any HTML file, even if it was created in a different application. Any advanced HTML codes not editable by Word will be left undisturbed, so you can edit in complete safety.

In this example we've opened a file created by a separate Web design package. Word will now let us edit its text, graphics and even the hyperlinks.

If you have been editing a file which has already been saved in .HTM format, you don't necessarily need to use the "Save as Web Page" option. A simple "Save" will suffice.

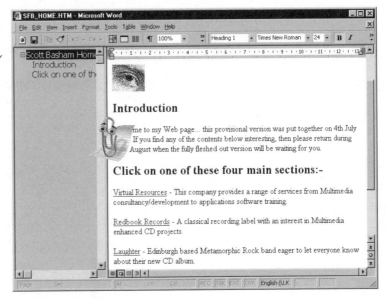

View HTML Source

This tool scores over a straight text editor in a number of ways. It allows you to see an organised view of your Web pages, and also uses a colour coding system to help you distinguish the syntax.

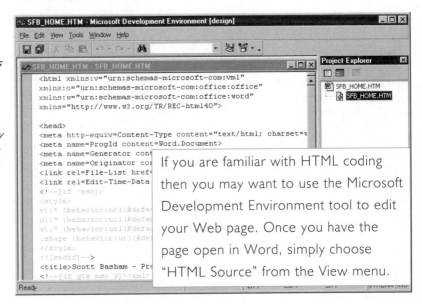

If you are familiar with HTML coding then you may want to use the Microsoft Development Environment tool to edit your Web page. Once you have the page open in Word, simply choose "HTML Source" from the View menu.

Using Word 2000 for E-mail

Using Word as Your E-mail Editor

If you use Microsoft Outlook or Exchange, your e-mail composition can be enhanced by many Word 2000 features such as spelling and grammar checking, version tracking and the use of tables.

To set up Word as E-mail Editor from Outlook

1 From Microsoft Outlook, open the Tools menu and choose Options.

2 Select the Mail Format tab and click on "Use Microsoft Word to edit e-mail messages".

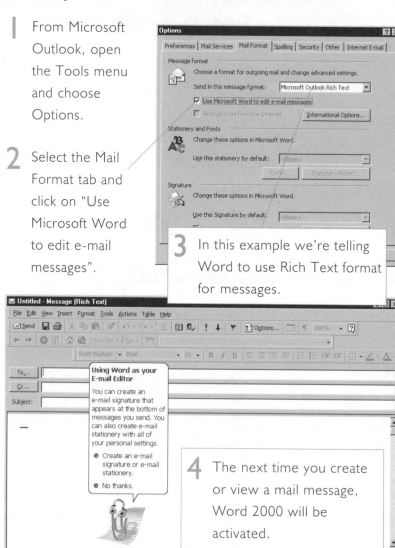

3 In this example we're telling Word to use Rich Text format for messages.

The first time you use Word 2000 for e-mail editing, the Office Assistant will offer you help with setting up an autosignature or stationery. These will be discussed on the next few pages.

4 The next time you create or view a mail message, Word 2000 will be activated.

Choosing Rich Text or HTML Format

Rich Text format allows many text formatting features (such as font, size, style and colour) to be used in e-mail messages. This is compatible with a wide range of e-mail applications.

Alternatively, you can choose HTML format, which will provide many more features including tables and graphics.

To use HTML as the Message Format

1 From Microsoft Outlook, open the Tools menu and choose "Options".

2 Choose HTML from the "Send in this message format" option.

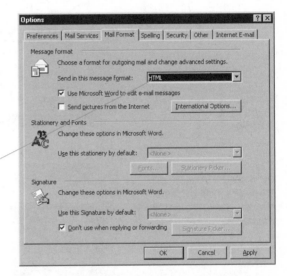

Look in the title bar if you want to check to see if the e-mail format is set to use Rich Text or HTML.

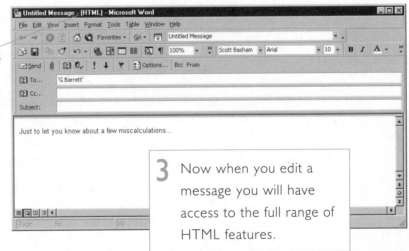

3 Now when you edit a message you will have access to the full range of HTML features.

E-mail Signatures

A special signature can be automatically added to the end of any e-mail message. This can contain text (including hyperlinks) or graphics.

| Go to the Tools menu and choose "Options". Select the General tab and click on the E-mail Options button.

2 Enter a name for your signature.

From the Personal Stationery tab you can choose a Theme for your messages. You can also set a specific font for new messages, and a separate font for replies or forwarded messages.

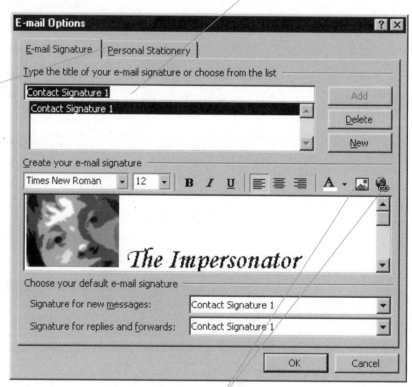

3 Type in its text. You can click on the Insert Picture or Insert Hyperlink buttons to add graphics or references to other pages.

4 Click on "Add".

The signature will now be available for any new messages you may send.

Advanced Topics

Word 2000 has many advanced features. Some are designed to generally make life easier while others let you enhance your documents with comments, tables of contents or even by compiling an index.

Covers

Chapter Twelve

The Reviewing Toolbar

Word 2000 incorporates several sophisticated features that allow you to review documents clearly, and track the various stages of these reviews. The Reviewing toolbar contains icons that allow you to access these features easily. It can be displayed in the normal way from the View menu.

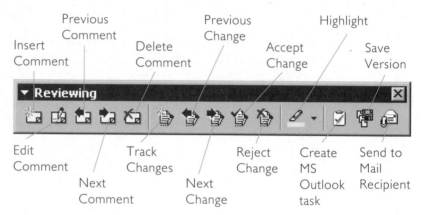

Inserting Comments

To insert a comment on a section of your document, do the following:

1 Highlight the text on which you wish to comment.

2 Click the Insert Comment icon.

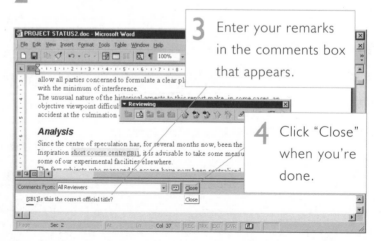

3 Enter your remarks in the comments box that appears.

4 Click "Close" when you're done.

Highlighting Text

If you want to mark a piece of text without appending any additional notes, you can highlight it, just as if you were using a real highlighter pen on paper. To do this, follow either of the steps below:

1 Select your text with the cursor tool, then click on the Highlighter icon.

If you use the highlighter icon's pop-up menu, then you can choose from a range of colours. Selecting "None" will remove the highlight altogether.

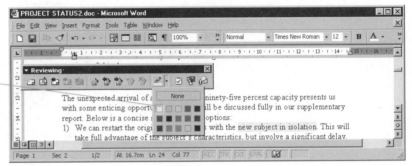

2 Alternatively click on the Highlighter icon first, to enter Highlighter mode, then highlight as many different pieces of text as you want. To return to normal text-editing mode, click on the Highlighter icon again.

Versioning

This is the facility to save the various stages of the evolution of a document, allowing you to see how its content has developed, and (if appropriate) which of the different authors of a document have made which changes. To save a new version of a document, do the following:

1 Click on the Save Version icon in the Reviewing toolbar.

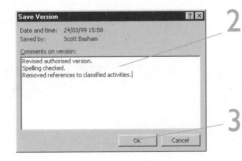

2 Enter your description of this version, and/or your comments on it, in this box.

3 Click "OK" to save the version.

To review the different versions of a document, follow these steps:

▌ Select "Versions" from the File menu.

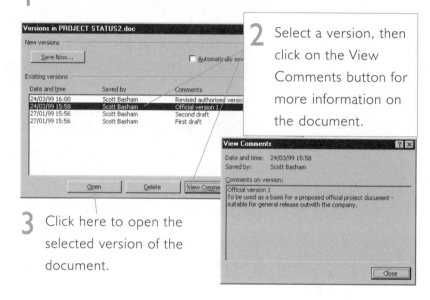

2 Select a version, then click on the View Comments button for more information on the document.

3 Click here to open the selected version of the document.

Macros

Macros are recordings of common activities. You can record your own Macros, and play them back whenever necessary.

Recording a Macro

▌ Go to the View menu, choose "Toolbars" and make sure that the Visual Basic Toolbar is active.

This gives you access to two buttons for recording and replaying Macros.

You can also access Macro recording and playback by opening the Tools menu and choosing Macros.

Run Macro   Record Macro

Visual Basic Editor (can be used for editing Macros on a command by command basis)

...cont'd

2 The Record Macro dialog box appears. Enter a name for your Macro. This must begin with a letter and can contain up to 80 letters and numbers. Spaces or special characters are not allowed.

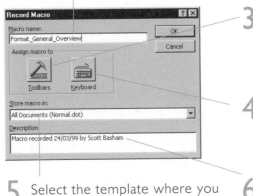

3 Click here to assign your new Macro to a toolbar.

4 Click here to assign your new Macro to a keyboard shortcut.

5 Select the template where you want to store the Macro.

6 Enter a description for your Macro.

You can also stop Macro recording by opening the Tools menu and choosing "Macros".

7 When you click OK, recording becomes active. You can now "walk through" the commands you wish to be included in the Macro. During this time your cursor takes the form of a pointer with a cassette tape attached. There is also a small toolbar which allows you to pause or stop recording:

8 When you have finished recording, click the Stop icon.

Running a Macro

You can run a Macro from a toolbar icon or keyboard shortcut if you chose either of these options when creating the Macro.

1 To play back a Macro, click the Play button and choose your Macro from the dialog box.

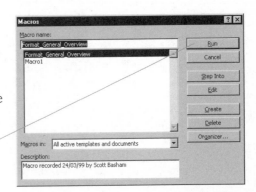

2 Click "Run".

Collaborating on Documents

If each of the different reviewers of a document works from a different computer, which is used by them alone, then there should be no need to alter the reviewer information as this should have been established when Word 2000 was installed. However, if a computer is shared by a number of people to review Word documents, then the user information should be changed whenever a reviewer begins, so that it is clear who made which comments.

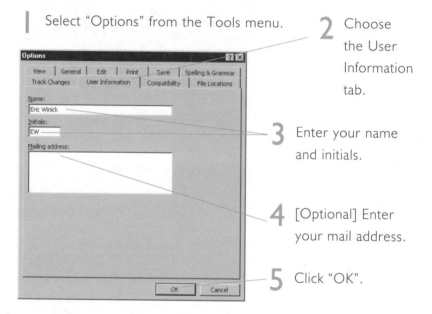

1 Select "Options" from the Tools menu.

2 Choose the User Information tab.

3 Enter your name and initials.

4 [Optional] Enter your mail address.

5 Click "OK".

Merging Documents

If a number of reviewers have been working together on the same document by updating the same Word file, then the sum of all their efforts is collected in the most up-to-date version of the document. However, if different reviewers have made changes to a document and saved the results as a different file (e.g., to take the document away to work on at home), it is possible to merge the files back into one document

1 With one of the files open, select Tools>Merge Documents.

2 In the file dialog that appears, double-click on the file to merge.

Text Boxes

Text boxes give you independent control over text flow and positioning as well as other attributes.

Inserting a new Text Box

1. Go to the Insert menu and choose "Text Box". You cursor will turn into a cross symbol.

2. Click and drag diagonally to create the Text Box.

The first thing you'll probably want to do is apply Text wrap to the new Text box. To do this, right-click on one of its edges and choose Format Text box. Activate the Layout tab.

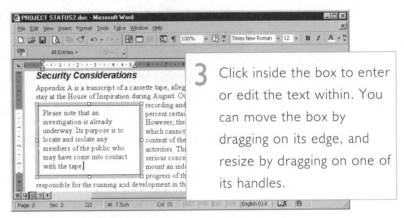

3. Click inside the box to enter or edit the text within. You can move the box by dragging on its edge, and resize by dragging on one of its handles.

The Text Box Toolbar

This gives you access to additional Text box options.

Break link   Previous text box   Next text box

Link text boxes   Change text direction

To link text boxes, click on the first box, then the Link button in the toolbar, then on the second box. Any text which doesn't fit in the first box will now flow automatically into the second.

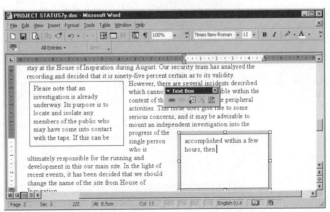

Footnotes and Endnotes

Word 2000 allows you to add footnotes (which appear at the bottom of a page), or endnotes (which appear at the end of your document). These reference text on the main page, usually using a superscript number.

1 Select the text which will reference the footnote or endnote, then choose "Footnote" from the Insert menu.

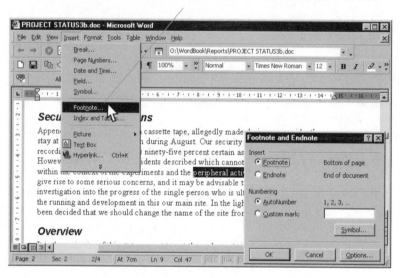

2 Choose Footnote/Endnote, a Numbering option, then click "OK".

Existing footnotes or endnotes are renumbered automatically each time you insert another.

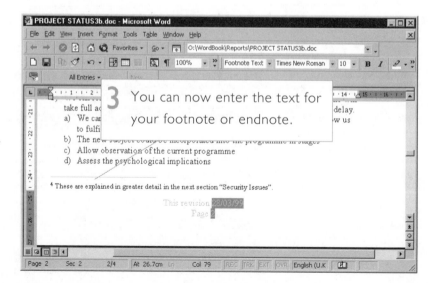

3 You can now enter the text for your footnote or endnote.

Tables of Contents

You can automatically create a Table of Contents for your document by asking Word 2000 to look for instances of particular styles, or entries that you create manually. Word will take care of tracking the page numbers of each entry.

Creating a new Table of Contents

1 Place your insertion point at a suitable location for your Table of Contents.

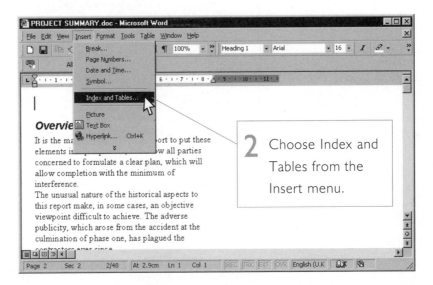

2 Choose Index and Tables from the Insert menu.

3 Make sure the Table of Contents tab is active.

4 Set the page and tab options.

By default, Word will use instances of the styles Heading 1, 2 and 3 to build the Table of Contents. You can change this by clicking on the Options button.

5 Choose a style from the Formats pop-up list then click "OK".

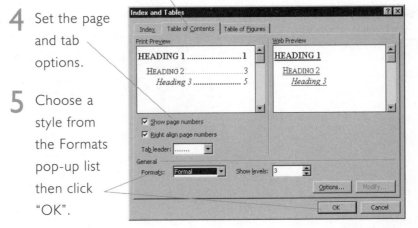

Word scans through your document for instances of different heading styles, and creates the Table of Contents.

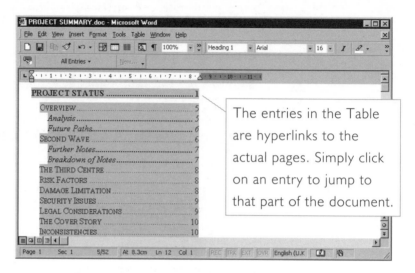

The entries in the Table are hyperlinks to the actual pages. Simply click on an entry to jump to that part of the document.

The grey background on the Table of Contents indicates that you're looking at a Word Field. Fields contain text which Word automatically generates. The background doesn't print, but you can change it by selecting "Options" from the Tools menu. Click on the View tab and choose a different option under Field shading.

Updating a Table of Contents

If you have added new headings, or edited your document so that the page numbers are different, then you'll probably want to update the Table of Contents to reflect the changes.

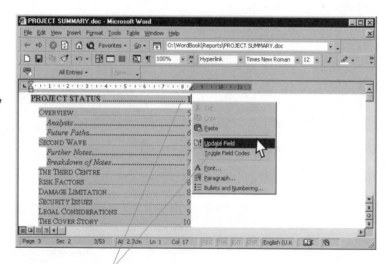

Right-click on the Table of Contents and choose Update Field from the pop-up menu.

...cont'd

If you have added or removed headings or Table of Contents entries, then you will need to choose Update entire table.

2 In the dialog box which appears, decide whether to update just the page numbers or to rebuild the whole table.

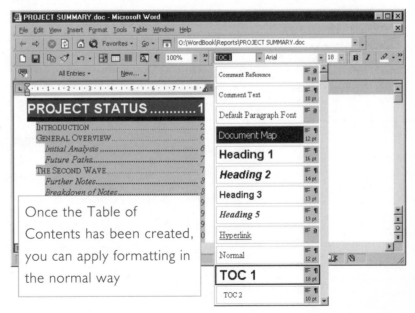

Any new entries now appear in the Table of Contents, and the page numbering is back in sync with the document

Entries in the Contents Table use special styles which have been set up automatically (they are named "TOC" plus a level number).

Any formatting changes you make normally affect these styles. This means that the new formatting will be retained even if you rebuild the Table of Contents.

Changing the Appearance of the Table of Contents

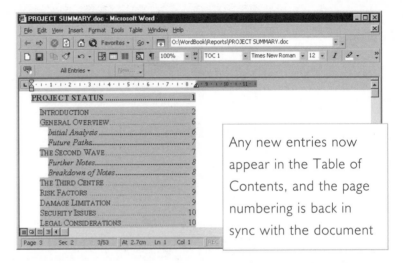

Once the Table of Contents has been created, you can apply formatting in the normal way

Adding a Manual Entry to the Table of Contents

Sometimes you may want to add an entry which does not use one of the Heading styles.

1 Click an Insertion Point in the relevant part of the document.

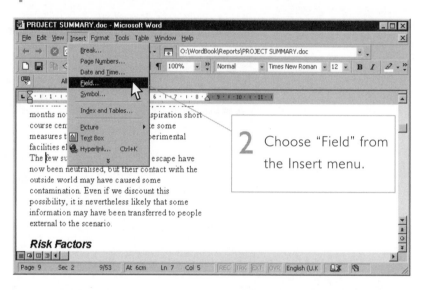

2 Choose "Field" from the Insert menu.

You can get Word to add the \l parameter for you by clicking on the Options button.

3 The Field dialog box appears. Under Categories, choose "Index and Tables".

4 For field names choose "TC".

5 "TC" will appear here. Add the text for the entry enclosed inside double quotes.

6 To set the entry at a particular level in the table, add a backslash followed by a lower case letter "l" then the level number.

7 Click "OK".

The field for the TOC entry is added to your document.

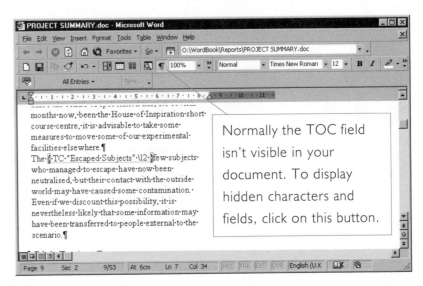

Normally the TOC field isn't visible in your document. To display hidden characters and fields, click on this button.

8 Now you need to rebuild the Table of Contents. Click to select your existing table, then choose "Index and Tables" from the Insert menu.

9 In the Index and Tables dialog, click the Options button.

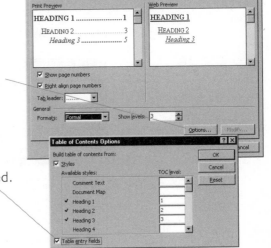

10 Make sure that "Table entry fields" is selected.

11 Click "OK" when asked if you want to replace the current Table of Contents.

Bookmarks

A Bookmark can help you keep track of a location in your document.

Bookmarks can be used to let you specify a range of pages when creating an index entry. See page 184 for more details.

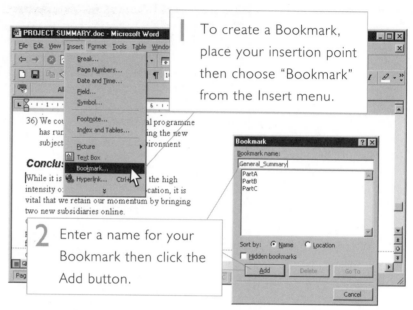

To create a Bookmark, place your insertion point then choose "Bookmark" from the Insert menu.

2 Enter a name for your Bookmark then click the Add button.

Indexing

Word 2000 makes the process of creating an index relatively straightforward.

Adding an Index entry

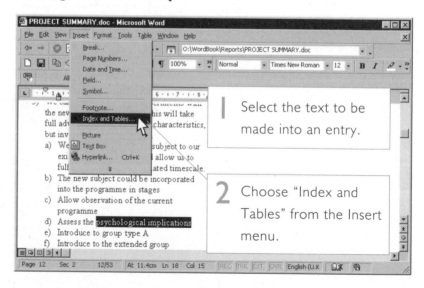

Select the text to be made into an entry.

2 Choose "Index and Tables" from the Insert menu.

The Index and Tables dialog box appears:

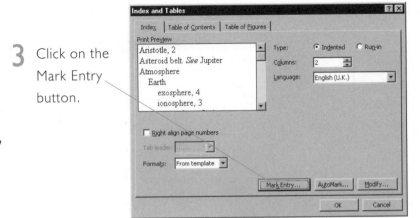

3 Click on the Mark Entry button.

The Mark Index Entry dialog stays open even after you've clicked the Mark button. This means that you can determine another index entry (by scrolling through your main document) then click the Mark button again, without having to go through the menus.

4 The Mark Index Entry dialog appears. If necessary, edit the text inserted in Main entry.

5 For a simple entry, leave the options set at Current Page and click on "Mark".

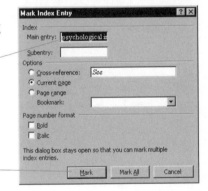

Topics and Subtopics

Most entries will probably only need to have text in the Main entry part of this dialog box.

However, if you want an index which includes topics and subtopics, then fill in the main topic under Main entry, then the subtopic under Subentry.

See the next page for an example of subtopics in an actual index.

Specifying Ranges of Pages

For most index entries you'll want just a single page number to appear. If you want a range of pages:

You can also create cross-reference entries. Click on the Cross-reference option and type in the relevant text for the entry.

1 Move to the end of the topic and create a bookmark (see page 182).

2 Locate the start of the topic and mark the index entry. Set the Options to Page range, and select your bookmark from the pop-up list.

Generating the Index

1 When you are ready, click an Insertion point where you'd like the Index to appear.

2 Go to the Insert menu and choose "Index and Tables".

3 Make sure the Index tab is active.

As with the Table of Contents, you can rebuild the Index at any time, or change its formatting by editing the styles (each named "Index" followed by a level number).

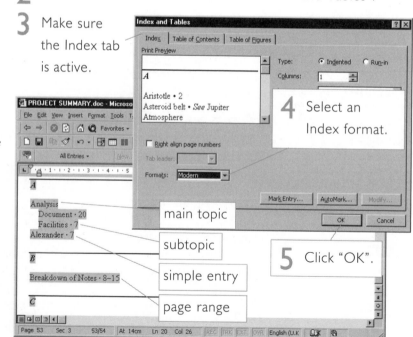

4 Select an Index format.

5 Click "OK".

main topic

subtopic

simple entry

page range

Language Autodetect

If you have multiple languages installed, Word 2000 can automatically select the correct language based on what you're currently typing.

Installing Multiple Languages

If you only have one language currently installed, you will need to install at least one more for the Language Autodetect feature to work.

1 Click on the Windows Start button, choose
Programs>Office Tools>Microsoft Office Language Settings.

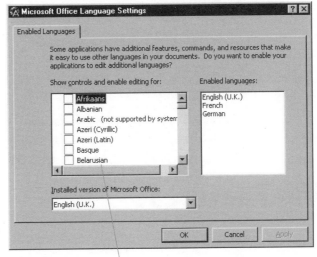

When you change the Microsoft Office Language Settings, Windows needs to shut down any Office Applications (such as Word). A dialog box will appear, offering to do this for you automatically.

2 To add a language, select it from the list on the left. Continue to select all the languages you require then click "OK" or apply.

3 Back in Word choose Tools>Language>Set Language. Make sure that "Detect language automatically" is switched on.

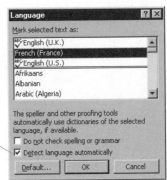

Compatibility Options

You can customise how Word displays documents which have been saved in another format.

These settings only affect how Word displays a document which has been saved in a particular format. It does not permanently change its formatting.

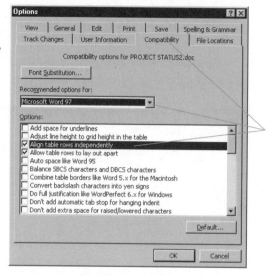

1 Go to the Tools menu and choose "Options".

2 Click on the Compatibility tab, select the file format and view or change its options.

Installing Features

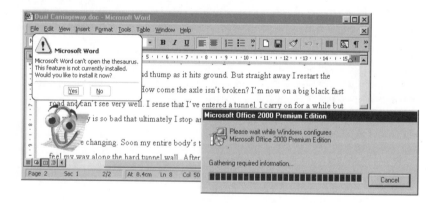

In order to conserve hard disk space, you can choose to include only the commonly used features when you first install Word. Later on, if you try to use a feature which isn't installed, Word will ask you if you want to load it there and then. If you answer "Yes", you'll need to insert your original CD. This feature is commonly known as "install on demand".

Index

L

M

N

O

P